The
Magisterial
Gaze

Manifest Destiny and American Landscape Painting c. 1830–1865

The Magisterial Gaze

Albert Boime

Smithsonian Institution Press • Washington and London

Editor: Lorraine Atherton
Designer: Linda McKnight
Production Editor: Kathryn Stafford

∞ The paper used in this publication meets the mini-
mum requirements of the American National Standard
for Permanence of Paper for Printed Library Materials
Z39.48–1984.

Printed in Hong Kong by South China Printing Company.

Cover: Jasper Francis Cropsey, *Autumn—On the Hudson
River*, 1860 (fig. 27, *infra*).

Library of Congress Cataloging-in-Publication Data

Boime, Albert.
    The magisterial gaze : manifest destiny and Ameri-
can landscape painting, c. 1830–1865 / by Albert Boime.
        p.   cm. — (New directions)
    Includes bibliographical references and index.
    ISBN 1-56098-095-8
    1. Landscape painting, American.   2. Landscape
painting—19th century—United States.   3. Messian-
ism, Political—United States—Influence.   I. Title.
II. Series: New directions (Smithsonian Institution
Press).
    ND1351.5.B65   1991
    758′.1′097309034—dc20   90-27719
                                                         CIP

Title page and opposite: Detail from Paul Frenzeny and
Jules Tavernier, *Denver from the Highlands*, 1874 (fig. 31,
infra).

Page 1 and opposite: Detail from Frederic Edwin Church,
Mount Ktaadn, 1853 (fig. 16, *infra*, and color plate).

For my mother and father, who moved West in pursuit of the American dream

Contents

Acknowledgments

I wish to express my gratitude to the following Smithsonian fellows and visiting scholars in residence at the National Museum of American Art for their help in the formulation of this essay: Eleanor Jones, Joni Kinsey, and Susan Sivard. Also at the NMAA, Elizabeth Broun and Lois Fink were constant sources of encouragement and support. Linda Bailey, Gerald Carr, Walter Dix, and Franklin Kelly also provided suggestions and expertise, for which I am grateful. Myra Boime heard me out and kept me on track, and I benefited from Robert Boime's insight into and passion for environmental issues. Eric Boime helped me locate important information on Gutzon Borglum, and Alan Wallach and Patricia Hills provided key bibliographic references. Ruth Kohn checked for errors at page-proof stage. Finally, I feel fortunate to have found in the staff of the Smithsonian Institution Press, including my editor Amy Pastan, designer Linda McKnight, manuscript editor Lorraine Atherton, Ruth Spiegel, and Kathy Stafford, a team committed to the highest quality at every level.

Preface

Earth Day, April 22, 1990. I am finishing the additions to this manuscript on the twentieth anniversary of the first Earth Day. We now understand that our current way of life cannot be perpetuated without grave damage to the planet and our own health. Ironically, by living out the nineteenth-century myth of progress (a term still sustained by Los Angeles real estate speculators who destroy to build bigger and higher) we have actually accomplished the opposite and demonstrated our antagonism to the earth. The will to mastery over the environment rather than the will to live in harmony may well prove to be our undoing. The theme of this book is how that will to mastery was articulated in landscape painting at the moment when it seized the imagination of the privileged elite.

The phrase "magisterial gaze" may have a Foucauldian ring about it (see especially M. Foucault, "The Eye of Power," *Power/Knowledge,* edited by C. Gordon, New York: Pantheon Books, 1980, pages 146–165), but the idea buzzed in my imagination before I had ever heard of Foucault. I began teaching the concept that the elevated point of view signified mastery over the land in my very first classes at the State University of New York at Stony Brook in 1968. Although I then argued the case rather crudely, I had already grasped the symbolic connection between the disciplined focus that submitted the vast reaches of the wilderness to an omniscient gaze and the larger national will to power in the form of Manifest Destiny. The insight into the indivisibility of imperialism and the destruction of the environment emerged with startling clarity that year. Gradually, the theory began to take on the contours of the present study, developing in response to the social movements of the sixties and surprising me by its capacity to comprehend the various ideological, social, scientific, and political phenomena that motivated the westward advance and helped lay the foundations of the American dream.

Yet little did I realize in 1968 that it held the key to understanding the prodigality of Americans in the environment. The idea that unlimited growth is attainable predisposed people in our society to leave unchecked the willingness to waste. The pioneer who cleared the woods, built a cabin, then sold it and moved on to the next site was the inadvertent forerunner of the modern speculator. Meanwhile, in the westward drive the Native Americans were either exterminated or shunted from one place to another. Only recently have we come to understand that they—like indigenous peoples everywhere—had a better grasp of the ecological issues than the European settlers. But they were stumbling blocks in the way of "progress"—read "short-term profits"—just as "greens" and mainstream environmentalist groups who now try to alert the public to the need for repairing the planet are perceived by the corporate chiefs as a bulwark against their expansionist plans. Currently the quaint-

sounding terms of "Manifest Destiny" (first
used by John L. O'Sullivan in his editorial in
the *United States Magazine, and Democratic Review* in 1845) and "expansionism" translate into
the immediate aim of multinational corpora-
tions to erase all trade barriers in a systematic
worldwide embrace of markets that would trans-
form the Third World into a cog of a globalis-
tic assembly line. The industrial boardrooms
whose willful negligence allowed refined petro-
leum to seep into the Monongahela River and
crude oil to soak Prince William Sound still
seek to view the world from the top, even if
now from their corporate towers. Harry Merlo,
the president of the Louisiana-Pacific Lumber
Company, spoke as heir to the nineteenth-
century expansionists when he stated in 1989:
"We log to infinity. Because we need it all. It's
ours. It's out there, and we need it all. Now."

The Magisterial Gaze

Manifest Destiny and American
Landscape Painting, c. 1830–1865

The privileged nineteenth-century American's experience of the sublime in the landscape occurred on the heights. The characteristic viewpoint of contemporary American landscapists traced a visual trajectory from the uplands to a scenic panorama below. Almost invariably the compositions were arranged with the spectator in mind, either assuming the elevated viewpoint of the onlooker or including a staffage figure seen from behind that functioned as a surrogate onlooker.[1] This Olympian bearing metonymically embraced past, present, and future, synchronically plotting the course of empire. The experience on the heights and its literary and aesthetic translation became assimilated to popular culture and remained and continues to remain a fundamental component of the national dream.[2] As such, it is inseparable from nationalist ideology. I will argue in this essay that there is an American viewpoint in American landscape painting that can be identified with this characteristic line of vision, and that this peculiar gaze represents not only a visual line of sight but an ideological one as well.

FOREGROUND AND BACKGROUND

The surge of scholarly interest in American landscape over the past three decades has been stimulated in part by the commercial and popular success of the New York school and the attempt to trace its roots to the tradition of the American sublime. The most recent studies tend in the direction of scientific and philosophic interpretations[3] and, more rarely, investigate the influence of patrons and social groups and contemporary political ideology.[4] Thus American scholarship has grounded the landscape tradition firmly in the literary, scientific, and political currents of the nineteenth century. What is now needed, I believe, is a comprehensive examination of the landscape from a theoretical perspective that can pull together the diverse strains of previous studies and establish a fresh synthesis.

In one of his Western short stories written at the turn of the century, Alfred Henry Lewis makes his protagonist declaim,

> The yawnin' peril to this nation, says Peets, as we're loiterin' over our drinks one Red light evenin', is the ignorance of the East. Thar's folks back thar, speshullay in Noo York, who with their oninstructed backs to the settin' sun, don't even know thar is a West. Likewise, they're proud as peacocks of their want of

knowledge. They'd feel plenty ashamed to be caught knowin' anything on the Rocky Mountain side of the Hudson River.[5]

Typical of those who romanticized the cowboy at the beginning of the Marlboro Man myth, Lewis was an Easterner himself who wrote his popular Wolfville tales in New York. As a journalist for a metropolitan readership, he profited from the progress he condemned. His conservatism was couched in a homespun dialect that indicted the East for its ignorance while knowing full well that this region had been primarily responsible for the territorial expansion across the Mississippi. Similarly, American writers and landscapists lamented "the axe of civilization" and the "ignorance and folly" that daily destroyed the garden, at the same time they were generating metaphors and pictorial systems proclaiming the course of empire.

The passage quoted above from "The Wisdom of Doc Peets" confronts the Hudson River with the Rocky Mountains, the geographical labels of the two most significant landscape schools of the last century. These distinctive cultural formations are inseparably linked to American national self-consciousness and its political expression in the form of Manifest Destiny. This aggressive ideology coincides with the new cosmopolitan respect for native scenery seen from an elevated perspective. When Lewis was writing, Frederick Jackson Turner broadcast his famous frontier thesis at a meeting of the American Historical Association held in Chicago at the Columbian World Exposition of 1893. In the context of an international fair, manifestly devoted to American domination and located at the gateway to the West, Turner struck up a theme that would have been familiar to every auditor. He suggested that his imaginary readers climb the Cumberland Water Gap, and from there looking westward they could view the United States "like a huge page in the history of society." As we read this continental page we find the record of social evolution:

> It begins with the Indian and hunter; it goes on to tell of the disintegration of savagery by the entrance of the trader, the pathfinder of civilization; we read the annals of the pastoral stage in ranch life; the exploitation of the soil by the raising of unrotated crops of corn and wheat in sparsely settled farming communities; the intensive culture of the denser farm settlement; and finally the manufacturing organization with city and factory system.[6]

Thus Turner's essay drew upon the literary and pictorial tradition to support his thesis of an increasing Americanization of culture commensurate with the shift westward. Analogously, the Hudson River school, which embodied that tradition, still contained residual elements of the European transit to the New World. The Euro-American dream of conquering an unspoiled and undeveloped terrain with the latest science and technology was realized in the railroad, which steamrolled the continent in the direction of an imagined authentic American civilization. Beginning around 1850 the idea of a transcontinental railway was promoted by boosters and businessmen east of the Mississippi. The several railway surveys in the 1850s embraced the kind of team one would expect to find on a colonial expedition to West Africa. Not fortuitously, many of the artists attached to the Western expeditions had been affiliated with the Hudson River school.

Most of this should be familiar to students of American culture, but until now there has been no systematic attempt to comprehend the landscape schools in a theoretical perspective through analysis of their formal structures and their significations. Thus far the most illuminating scholarly research in the realm of landscape has emphasized the relation of landscape painting to the myths of the wilderness and the West in terms of historical narrative and content.[7] The myth of nature and its conversion into religious doctrine has centered on the need to resolve the antinomy between nature and culture, between the Virgin Land and its deflowering. In this scenario the painters are reduced to impotent spectators passively documenting a passing scene. I intend to argue just the opposite, that far from being passive recorders they participated in the very system they condemned and projected it symbolically in their work. Their view from the summit metaphorically undercut the past and blazed a trail into the wilderness for "the abodes of commerce and seats of manufactures."[8]

Relying on a few key monuments and texts, I hope to demonstrate that the landscape view from the heights—from the simplest topographical description to the most grandiose machine—unites the Hudson River, Luminist, and Rocky Mountain schools, revealing in their common structural paradigm the sociopolitical ideology of expansionist thought. The period studied is bracketed by the opening of the Erie Canal in 1825 and the termination of the Civil War in 1865, the epoch of the country's greatest territorial conquests. By emphasizing the *langue* rather than the *parole* of this tradition, I hope to resolve some of the many problems centering on the opposition of the machine and the garden and at the same time provide a framework for comprehending current research on critical but fragmentary aspects of American landscape painting, including patronage, geology, scientific illustration, and Western survey and railway expeditions.

American landscape, like American consciousness in general, is the product of an Anglo-European immigrant imagination. If other ethnic groups had a more legitimate claim to its physical and mental space, their contribution in a real sense has been colonized and assimilated to the dominant mentality. Those who dwelled in American lands before the arrival of the explorers and fur traders or those who came here involuntarily were deprived of their being and status and forced to surrender their cultural heritage for the sake of the dominant sign system. The spectacle and entertainment potential of Native American and African American culture were the spoils of war and repression.

Yet if it was the Western Europeans who dreamed the American dream, it was they who could best understand its underlying dynamic.

The aristocratic Alexis de Tocqueville, shocked by the July Revolution and predisposed to discover the pitfalls of democracy, became conscious of the inevitable destruction that gave

> so peculiar a character and such a touching beauty to the solitudes of America. One sees them with a melancholy pleasure; one is in some sort of hurry to admire them. Thoughts of the savage, natural grandeur that is going to come to an end become mingled with splendid anticipations of the triumphant march of civilization. One feels proud to be a man, and yet at the same time one experiences I cannot say what bitter regret at the power that God has granted us over nature.[9]

Some twenty-five years later, another Frenchman, the radical geographer Elisée Reclus, looked upon the American experience with profound bitterness. For him it was a vast auction house where everything is sold, "slaves and master above market price, votes and honor, the Bible, and consciences. Everything belongs to the highest bidder." And he continued:

> I often ask myself, stupefied in face of this America so respected *abroad,* so little respectable inside, where is the necessary progress that every people must accomplish in its evolution? It is truly said that everything here reduces to a development in space, carried out by this unceasing migration from the Atlantic to the Pacific, to a progress in time, since the American enters active life at the moment of birth, and to a progress in which is the vegetative life of the human being, since all have a piece of bread in the tooth. But the larger progress is almost totally independent of their will, this progress is forced as a result of new relations between man and earth and races to races; because these new relations have posed humanity with new questions that are necessary to resolve one way or the other. [10]

Thus both the conservative and the radical grasped the contradictions at the heart of the new American society, contradictions essentially rooted in their own expectations and disillusionments. These contradictions devolve on the notion of futurity and progress, which is the hallmark of the American dream but which in the realization induces reflections on decadence and destruction.

The contradictions perceived by the Europeans in stark terms could also be glimpsed by the Americans of the transition. Thomas Cole, for example, could write in his popular "Essay on American Scenery" that "looking over the yet uncultivated scene, the mind's eye may see far into futurity. Where the wolf roams, the plough shall glisten; on the gray crag shall rise temple and tower—mighty deeds shall be done in the new pathless wilderness; and poets unborn shall sanctify the soil." [11] At the same time, Cole decried the disappearance of the wilderness and the interposition of the mercantile mentality between human beings and nature. He experienced this contradiction in his own soul because he profited from the mercantile mentality as one of the poets who sanctified the soil. Indeed, as we shall see, it was his ability to encode in his landscape the idea of futurity and progress that made his work so saleable. To decry the despoiling of the wilderness was to indict not just the bankers and land developers but his own imaginative projections and landscape paradigm. Hence the losing game played by the Americans: on the one hand, their conditions for success depended on the razing of the wilderness and the cultivation of a splendid civilization, while with each inch of cultivated soil a little piece of their innocence disappeared. There was no way not to glorify the material development as progress, and there was no way to avoid condemning its results. The realization of the American dream implied the total corruption of the dreamer. Hence the paradoxical qualities of Cole's cyclical *Course of Empire,* which traces the rise and fall of a nation, a diachronic breakdown of the dream endlessly replayed.[12]

As in the *Course of Empire* series, Cole's projection invariably originates at an elevation from which one can survey the panorama below. His *River in the Catskills,* painted in 1843, exemplifies his approach (Fig. 1). A young farmer standing in for the spectator leans on his axe and gazes from a hilltop foreground across the wide vista below. The foreground is strewn with thickets and storm-blasted trees symbolizing the undomesticated landscape that the farmer prepares to clear. We follow his gaze from the boundary of the wilderness across the river to the cultivated middleground zone and the farm dwellings. Moving perpendicularly to the youth's line of vision is a train in the middle distance crossing a bridge. The line of vision extends into the remote distance where smoke arises from scarcely seen manufactories

Fig. 1. Thomas Cole, *River in the Catskills*, 1843. Gift of Martha C. Karolik for the M. and M. Karolik Collection of American Paintings, 1815–1865. Courtesy, Museum of Fine Arts, Boston.

on the horizon. Cole's picture tells us that the future lies over the horizon, with time here given a spatial location. Just two years later, an Illinois congressman named John Wentworth declared that God designed the original states "as the great center from which civilization, religion, and liberty should radiate and radiate until the whole continent shall bask in their blessing."

Of course, in actuality, the farmer would be facing in the opposite direction, away from the boundary of civilization toward the forest wilderness to be cleared. I see this reversal, however, as a metaphorical mirror of the pioneer's vision of the future prospects awaiting him. In looking backward, the farmer declares from the edge between wilderness and savagery on the one hand, civilization and order on the other, that progress moves along the timeline of the landscape. What he sees in effect is the process of domestication in progress, an ideal to behold during the actual drudgery of clearing the ugly remnants of the wilderness. This is strikingly evident in a design for a bank-note engraving of 1852 that depicts a farmer clearing the woods with his axe, his body facing in the direction of the viewer and hence the wilderness with the summit view and middle landscape behind him (Fig. 2). He pauses in his work to glance behind him at the fruits of his labor, gazing downhill at the log cabin dwelling and cultivated land.

This perspective is so pervasive in the art and literature of nineteenth-century America that we have to see it as an encoding of a solution to the American dilemma. In his seminal essay entitled "Nature," Emerson wrote with the upland vista in mind:

The charming landscape which I saw this morning is indubitably made up of some twenty or thirty farms. Miller owns this field, Locke that, and Manning the woodland be-

Fig. 2. Anonymous, bank-note engraving, Rawdon, Wright, Hatch and Edson, 1852. Prints and Photographs Division, Library of Congress, Washington, D.C.

yond. But none of them owns the landscape. There is a property in the horizon which no man has but he whose eye can integrate all the parts, that is, the poet.[13]

Emerson here associates himself with the Promethean pioneers bringing light and imposing order on the unruly land surface. Although he attains mastery through aesthetic and literary metaphor, his urge to subjugate and control nature beyond his neighbors' boundaries coincides with the expansionist mood of the national imagination. As he noted in the same essay:

Every spirit builds itself a house, and beyond its house a world, and beyond its world a heaven. Know then that the world exists for you. . . . All that Adam had, all that Caesar could, you have and can do. Adam called his house, heaven and earth, Caesar called his house, Rome; you perhaps call yours, a cob-bler's trade; a hundred acres of ploughed land; or a scholar's garret. Yet line for line and point for point your dominion is as great as theirs, though without fine names. Build therefore your own world.[14]

Emerson's essay consistently invokes an observer with a unique point of view and in a significant passage declares that every appearance in nature corresponds to a particular state of mind. That state of mind can only be articulated by referring to the natural appearance as a metonymic image. Thus the landscape horizon and all of its natural history will be married to human history. His example, "visible distance behind and before us, is respectively our image of memory and hope," attests to the use of geographical metaphors to suggest past, present, and future.[15]

William Cullen Bryant was another crucial figure who attempted to define an elite independent American culture in the nineteenth century, and in addition to his pervasive impact on the writers, his influence on Cole, Asher B. Durand, and Thomas Doughty makes him one of the founders of the first indigenous school of American landscape painting. Like the Hudson River artists, he sought the heights for inspiration, making frequent excursions to the Palisades on the west side of the Hudson and to the Ramapo Mountains, the Berkshires, and the Catskills.[16] Poems such as "Thanatopsis," "The Flood of Years," and "Monument Mountain" contain metaphors for liberating mental horizons inseparably linked with the panoramic viewpoint.[17] His poetic vision is closely integrated with mountain metaphors identifying personal and national aspiration with the extensive view from the summit. In "Monument Mountain," Bryant advises his reader:

Thou who wouldst see the lovely and the wild
Mingled in harmony on Nature's face,
Ascend our rocky mountains. Let thy foot
Fail not with weariness, for on their top
The beauty and the majesty of earth,
Spread wide beneath, shall make thee to forget
The steep and toilsome way. There, as thou
　　stand'st,
The haunts of men below thee, and around
The mountain summits, thy expanding heart
Shall feel a kindred with that loftier world
To which thou art translated, and partake
The enlargement of thy vision.[18]

This vista encompasses the solitudes yet untouched by culture, but it is mainly "the haunts of men"—white villages, herds, and swarming roads—to which the eye is drawn.

Soon Bryant recalls the sad legend of the lovesick Indian maiden who threw herself from the mountaintop, an association born of his desire to reconcile his panoramic projection of the progress of American civilization with the tragic destruction of the Native American population. In "A Walk at Sunset" he identifies "the glories of a dying day" with the memory of "the hunter tribes" now vanished from the scene, "gone as thy setting blaze / Goes down the west, while night is pressing on." As he looks out over the transformation of the former wilderness, he muses:

> Yon field that gives the harvest, where the
>   plough
> Strikes the bare bone, is all that tells their story
>   now.

Bryant recognizes that his own sense of triumph and the source of his poetic inspiration are predicated on the suppression of the native peoples.

I stand upon their ashes in thy beam,
The offspring of another race, I stand,
Beside a stream they loved, this valley-stream.

Yet he reaffirms the national progress as part of a larger historical necessity in his final salute to the setting sun:

> Farewell! but thou shalt come again—thy light
>   Must shine on other changes, and behold
> The place of the thronged city still as night—
>   States fallen—new empires built upon the
>   old—
> But never shalt thou see these realms again
> Darkened by boundless groves, and roamed by
>   savage men.[19]

Bryant identified his own material interests with the futurity of American ascendance. In the midst of real estate negotiations for a hillside location overlooking Long Island

Sound, he wrote his brother John on 5 February 1843: "Congratulate me! There is a probability of my becoming a landholder in New York! I have made a bargain for about forty acres of solid earth at Hemstead Harbor, on the north side of Long Island."[20] That same year he threw himself behind the Senate bill providing for the extension of U.S. laws into new territory; in his editorial of January 6 for the New York *Evening Post* he wrote,

> It is a duty which the United States owes to mankind, to assert inflexibly its title to its proper territory, to guard it religiously from all encroachments by the powers of Europe, that it may become the home of men living under democratic institutions, framed after the pattern of our own. . . . We have no right to give up a foot of the domain in which Providence has put under our charge, to the evils of a colonial, or an aristocratic government. We should early mark out our just limits, and take early

measures to hold them sacred against the invasion of the governments of the old world.[21]

Three years later, Walt Whitman, another young editor with a panoramic grasp of affairs, advocating that the U.S. keep "a fast grip on California," disingenuously exclaimed, "We love to indulge in thoughts of the future extent and power of this republic—because with its increase is the increase of human happiness and liberty."[22] An active agent of Manifest Destiny, Whitman saw in the Mexican War a golden opportunity "to furnish a cluster of new stars for the spangled banner."[23] His editorial "American Futurity" prophesies that thirty years hence "America will be confessed the *first nation* on the earth. We of course mean that her power, wealth, and the happiness and virtue of her citizens will then obtain a pitch which other nations cannot favorably compare with. . . . The mind is lost in contemplating such incalculable acres."[24] Taking the broad view from the summit, Whitman examined the western territory.

> Stretching between the Alleghany Mountains and the Pacific Ocean, are killions of uncultivated acres of land—long rolling prairies—interminable savannahs, where the fat earth is covered with grass reaching to a height unknown in our less prolific north—forests, amid whose boughs nothing but silence reigns. . . . The mind becomes almost lost in tracing in imagination those hidden and boundless tracts of our territory.[25]

Then, like the typical "expectant capitalist," he forecasts the transformation of this wilderness into empire:

> We lose ourselves in the anticipation of what may be seen there in future times—the flourishing cities, the happy family homes, the stately edifices of public improvement, the sights and sounds of national prosperity.

Here is a dynamic source of intellectual energy for both his poetry and prose, the force behind his imaginative rendering of the amplitude of space and extensive prospects. Even when more disillusioned than hopeful, he could title his most serious contribution to prose literature "Democratic Vistas," with its poignant clarification: "Far, far, indeed, stretch, in distance, our Vistas!" After having financed his most creative years through the buying and selling of real estate, he could aestheticize Manifest Destiny from the elevated vantage point in the most optimistic terms. The protagonist of *Leaves of Grass* soars breathlessly across the continent like John Gast's Spirit of American Progress, embracing all of its varied geography and its teeming life from coast to coast. As in the Hudson River landscapes, past, present, and future are synchronically merged in a cosmic present.

Less all-embracing than Whitman, Fitz-Greene Halleck, a merchant-poet attached to the Knickerbocker Club, took the panoramic view as an extension of personal and patriotic power. He spoke for the Wall Street crowd in his celebration of Manhattan as seen from his Weehawken hillside villa in the poem "Fanny":

Amid thy forest solitudes he climbs
   O'er crags, that proudly tower above the deep,
And knows that sense of danger which sublimes
   The breathless moment—when his daring step
Is on the verge of the cliff, and he can hear
The low dash of the wave with startled ear.
. . . .
In such an hour he turns, and in his view,
   Ocean, and earth, and heaven, burst before
      him;
Clouds slumbering at his feet, and the clear blue
   Of summer's sky in beauty bending o'er him—

The city bright below; and far away,
Sparkling in golden light, his own romantic bay.

Tall spire, and glittering roof, and battlement,
   And banners floating in the sunny air;
And white sails o'er the calm blue waters bent,
   Green isle, and circling shore, are blended
      there
In wild reality. When life is old,
And many a scene forgot, the heart will hold

Its memory of this; nor lives there one
   Whose infant breath was drawn, or boyhood's
      days
Of happiness were passed beneath that sun,
   Tied in his manhood's prime can calmly gaze
Upon that bay, or on that mountain stand,
Nor feel the prouder of his native land. [26]

Warmly attached to Bryant, James Fenimore Cooper, Washington Irving, N. P. Willis, and the landscapist Asher B. Durand, Halleck shares their devotion to cliffside metaphors apotheosizing the national culture and their triumphant place within it.

The same attitude is expressed in the writings of Thoreau, an inveterate mountain climber who noted in a journal entry of 20 October 1852:

> Many a man, when I tell him that I have been on to a mountain, asks if I took a glass with me. No doubt, I could have seen further with a glass, and particular objects more distinctly—could have counted more meeting-houses; but this has nothing to do with the peculiar beauty and grandeur of the view which an elevated position affords. It was not to see a few particular objects, as if they were near at hand, as I had been accustomed to see them, that I ascended the mountain, but to see an infinite variety far and near in their relation to each other, thus reduced to a single picture.[27]

While on the surface this seems like a reasonable aesthetic statement, on closer inspection we see that the wish to reduce the panorama "to a single picture" implies a will to power and control, which eliminates from the broad picture the finicky details that contradict and despoil the whole.

But the need to ascend to catch a glimmer of the whole without the details brings with it the same anxieties and same contradictions glimpsed at the level of the horizon. In his journal entry for 29 October 1857 Thoreau describes a recurrent dream that takes place in the mountains:

> The perfect mountain height is already thoroughly purified. It is as if you trod with awe the face of a god turned up, unwittingly but helplessly, yielding to the laws of gravity. And are these not such mountains, east or west, from which you may look down on Concord in your thought, and on all the world? In dreams I am shown this height from time to time, and

I seem to have asked my fellow once to climb there with me, and yet I am constrained to believe that I never actually ascended it. It chances, now I think of it, that it rises in my mind where lies the Burying-Hill. You might go through its gate to enter that dark wood, but that hill and its graves are so concealed and obliterated by the awful mountain that I never thought of them as underlying it. Might not the graveyards of the just always be hills, ways by which we ascend and over look the plain?[28]

Clearly, mountain climbing for Thoreau was no simple physical exercise but corresponded to deep-seated mental traits, which he rationalized with philosophical divagations. His dream concerned death, and the act of climbing the mountain was the means of transcending it, of entering a divine realm and delighting in the opportunity of overlooking the plain, that is, having the perspective of the godhead. Elsewhere he noted that "simple races" like "sav-

ages" do not climb mountains; mountaintops are sacred and fearsome tracts inhabited by spirits hostile to human interlopers. Thoreau concluded that "only daring and insolent men, perchance, go there,"[29] in other words, Europeans mastering the New World and rivaling the gods with their awesome results. He himself experiences this heady sense of omnipotence in the mountains, asking himself in an exalted mood at one point: "What is this Titan that has possession of me?"[30]

It is this spiritual uplift he feels at the summit of Wachusett in July 1842:

There was little of the sublimity and grandeur which belong to mountain scenery [i.e., of the Ruskin variety], but an immense landscape to ponder on a summer's day. We could see how ample and roomy is nature. As far as the eye could reach there was little life in the landscape; the few birds that flitted past did not crowd. The travelers on the remote highways, which intersect the country on every side, had no fellow-travelers for miles, before or behind. On every side, the eye ranged over successive circles of towns, rising one above another, like the terraces of a vineyard, till they were lost in the horizon. Wachusett is, in fact, the observatory of the State. There lay Massachusetts, spread out before us in its length and breadth, like a map.[31]

Thus Thoreau, like the good surveyor that he was, gains control of the land reduced to the metaphorical level of a map. Indeed, Wachusett revealed to him the larger Appalachian range, a northeast-to-southwest chain that guided American migration of settlers charting the course of national destiny.

Thoreau, the seeker of solitudes, cannot help musing on future settlements in the most obscure sites, as if this musing itself were some form of creative rumination. Close to the summit of Katahdin, the highest mountain in Maine, he espied his companions on the side of the peak gathering cranberries, which stimulated thoughts on the possible economic future of the zone below:

When the country is settled and roads are made, these cranberries will perhaps become an article of commerce. From this elevation, just on the skirts of the clouds, we could overlook the country west and south for a hundred miles. There it was, the State of Maine, which we had seen on the map, but not much like that. Immeasurable forest to shine on, that eastern *stuff* we hear of in Massachusetts. No clearing, no house. It did not look as if a solitary traveller had cut so much as a walking-stick there. . . . It was a large farm for somebody, when cleared.[32]

Here Thoreau's creative imagination is inseparable from the power granted him on the heights, a power ultimately rooted in his sense of imaginative control of the land.

It is this gaze of command, or commanding view—as it was so often termed in the nineteenth-century literature—that I will call the magisterial gaze, the perspective of the American on the heights searching for new worlds to conquer. It presupposes the spectator as sightseer on the ledge or crest subjugating the boundless reality to a disciplined scrutiny and simultaneously taking a reading from this orientation that is profoundly personal and ideological at the same time. The panoramic prospect becomes a metonymic image—that is, it embodies, like a microcosm, the social and political character of the land—of the desire for dominance. I use this term to distinguish it from the North European viewpoint, particularly as it is manifested in the work of the German painter Caspar David Friedrich. Friedrich's landscape perspectives are generally organized from the opposing perspective that I call the reverential gaze. Typically, his point of view moves upward from the lower picture plane and culminates on or near a distant mountain peak (Fig. 3). Often the beholder is cued to

Fig. 3. Caspar David Friedrich, *Tetschner Altar, or The Cross in the Mountains,* 1808. Staatlich Gemäldegalerie Neue Meister, Dresden.

this ascending trajectory by *Rückenfiguren*, one or two figures seen from the rear with whom the beholder must identify. The reverential gaze signified the striving of vision toward a celestial goal in the heavens, starting from a wide, panoramic base. (One way to imagine this is to picture an upended cone with the apex tilted away from the viewer.) The convergence of the line of vision on the celestial focal point metaphorically implied the yearning for the unity of the German nation under God.[33]

That is precisely the inverse of the American gaze. In American works the apex of the imaginary cone is the eye of the presumed beholder already established at the summit; from there the cone takes in the panorama below. In this sense, the beholder occupies the spatial location assigned to the Godhead in Friedrich's work. The magisterial gaze assumes a perspective akin to the divine, represented in the Masonic-influenced Great Seal of the United States, in which the symbol of the Novus Ordo Seclorum is the radiant eye coterminous with the apex of the pyramid (Fig. 4). The same concept operates in Gutzon Borglum's colossal heads carved out of the summit of Mount

Fig. 4. The Great Seal of the United States. Reproduced on verso of a dollar bill.

Rushmore, with Jefferson's gaze deliberately directed westward from a point once sacred to the Dakota Indians.

The principle is also dramatically demonstrated in Seth Eastman's popular manual on topographical drawing, adapted in West Point's curriculum early in the nineteenth century.[34] In the lesson on the method of converting a ground plan seen from a bird's-eye prospect into a perspectival scheme with the actual eye of the beholder substituting for the vanishing point above the horizon, the diagrams take on allegorical as well as technical significance.[35] The first design presupposes the spectator-artist on a hill sighting on the objects, while the second assumes the reverse, with the symbolic eye of the beholder now sighting down from the celestial zone (Fig. 5). At the same time, the rays of the visual cone are also reversed in the two diagrams, with the first line of sight bisecting the wide angle emanating from the

viewpoint of the beholder seen from the rear, while in the second the orthogonals converge on the eye comprehending that portion of the plan falling within the first angle. The second part of the schematic design shows the line of sight equivalent to the height of the eye above the horizontal plane. Thus even in the practical treatises the magisterial gaze manifests itself in both symbolic and instrumental guise.

Of course other nationalities have experienced and expressed similar feelings on the heights: Swiss (Salomon Gessner, Bénédict de Saussure, and Jean-Jacques Rousseau), German (Goethe), English (Lord Byron, J. M. W. Turner, and John Ruskin), to name only a few.[36] But nowhere else do we find such a major body of visual and literary texts sharing a spatial and chronological coherence and constituting a collective expression of the "peak" experience. It is this systematic projection of the unlimited horizons as a metonymic image of

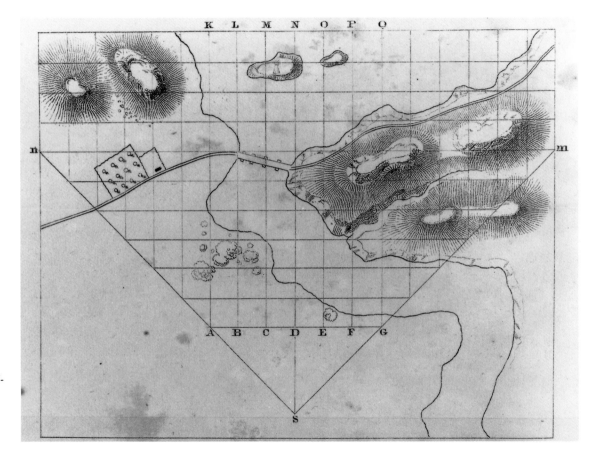

Fig. 5. Method of drawing a perspective view from a topographical plan, 1837. Reproduced in *Treatise on Topographical Drawing*, by Seth Eastman (New York: Wiley and Putnam), Plate 6.

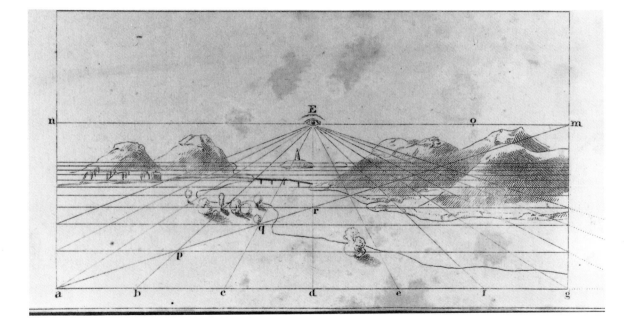

America's futurity that makes this body of material unique in its geographical, national, and temporal setting. It is not unique in its appeal to and hold over the individual imagination but rather in its manifestation as the collective and characteristic expression of the privileged national ideal, the ruling-class aspiration for American society that still endures. [37]

That the magisterial gaze implied for Americans something inherent in their culture is hinted at in Nathaniel Hawthorne's *The Marble Faun* (1860). When the American sculptor, Kenyon, visits Count Donatello's country villa situated on a height over a broad expanse of valley, he is struck by the house's fortresslike tower, which is the most prominent object in the landscape. Kenyon's fascination for the tower and his impatience to climb it are misunderstood by Donatello, who is indifferent to it. When Kenyon obtains the summit, he

"felt as if his being were suddenly magnified a hundredfold; so wide was the Umbrian valley that suddenly opened before him." Kenyon's eye sweeps across the spacious map and passes from the rural to the urban tracts, following the meandering path of a gleaming river. "It seemed as if all Italy lay under his eyes in that one picture." Significantly, the vista recalled to Kenyon's mind "the fondly remembered acres of his father's homestead." Hence the image of vastness in the aristocratic Italian setting is transposed to American patriarchal authority.

In an impassioned expression of gratitude to his host for providing the opportunity to glimpse the majestic scene, Kenyon translates the experience into spiritual uplift, comparing the climb to an ascent "into the higher regions of emotion and spiritual enjoyment," whose concrete embodiment are the "grand hieroglyphics" of the expansive landscape. The ascent is further rationalized as a leap above "the common level" and a "wider glimpse of [God's] dealings with mankind!" Kenyon now shifts from the actual topographical data to an abstract plane that essentially identifies his father's authority over the land with the transcendental control of the Godhead. Finally, these insights are seen as peculiarly American: Donatello throws up his hands in frustration, "striving with unwonted grasp to catch the analogies which so cheered his friend," and the Italian gloomily confesses, "You discern something that it is hidden from me."[38]

The theme trickled down into the popular literature as well. In the dime-novel Westerns produced by the publishing house of Beadle and Adams, the tension between expansionist utopian and primitivist thought in the face of the receding wilderness was played out with monotonous frequency.[39] Typically, each narrative of individual heroism participates in the larger historical process in which human beings move ineluctably westward, reducing the wilderness and replacing it with an industrious civilization. Inevitably, the extermination of Native Americans is tied to the conquest of the wilderness and its transformation into an Edenic garden. Edward S. Ellis's popular *Seth Jones; or, The Captives of the Frontier* (1860) begins straightaway with the pioneer in a settlement musing on the westward tide and foreseeing that "villages and cities would take the place of the wild forest, while the Indians would be driven further on towards the setting sun."[40]

Foresight and elevation are conceptually inseparable in tracing this development. In Edward Willett's *The Hunted Life; or, The Outcasts of the Border* (1867), a veteran hunter and his spouse stand on the crest of a Kentucky mountain range and envision the future site of a pastoral society.[41] Dime novelists consistently write of the wilderness as potential paradise, no matter what geographical site they are describing. At the same time, they also express the sense of loss that this entails. Frederick Whittaker's *Boone, the Hunter; or, The Backwoods Belle* (1873) has the irrepressible pioneer, formerly the hero of civilization, now lament the transformation he heralded. Standing on a hilltop with his brother, he gazes over a virgin plain:

> "Squire," he said softly, "when first I stood on this hill and looked out over the plains of this favored land, five strong brave men stood by me, and we rejoiced together that the Lord had shown us such a goodly heritage. Brother, of those five not one is left, and only I am alive to tell the people of the Yadkin what manner of land this is, and how I was preserved. And yet, brother, I am loth to depart from it and bring back settlers. A few years more, and yonder forest will lie low, while of all that great herd of God Almighty's cattle, not one will be found this side of the great river. The ax and the rifle will turn paradise into a market for men to buy and sell, and you and I brother, where shall we be?"[42]

Thus the Boone of the dime novel verifies the assimilation of the magisterial gaze into the popular consciousness of the American public, following it along the line of futurity on the one hand while reflecting on the civilization hard on his back. The mythical features of paradise are found to be contradictory in promising utopia where utopia already exists.

The pictorial realization of the magisterial gaze developed more slowly than its textual counterpart, as is seen in the earliest of the Hudson River albums, William G. Wall's *Hudson River Port Folio* of 1828.[43] Wall's descriptions of the plates anticipate those of the later writers: although the portfolio purports to be a detached study of key picturesque sites along the river, real estate pushes itself to the foreground of Wall's discussions. Reporting on

Little Falls at Luzerne, Wall does not fail to note that the "large house on the rock belongs to Mr. Rockwell, a gentleman of property." The text for Plate II, *The Junction of the Sacandaga and Hudson Rivers,* espies two prominent homes "assuming a proud pre-eminence over the rest of the struggling hamlet." Yet if the beholder cannot fail to observe the "commanding view" of these mansions, the directional gaze in both plates is the opposite of what one would expect (Figs. 6, 7).

Wall's sympathies were with the elite landowners who alone could have afforded his costly portfolio. When describing the vicinity around Baker's Falls (Plate VIII), he laments the absence of advanced agricultural industry and pleads for a major effort on the part of "the wealthier and more educated" segment of society to introduce "better principles than those by which the great mass of our farmers are regulated." Here again he attests to a particular

historical moment, when the professional and merchant classes began purchasing country estates, organized agricultural societies, and imposed more intensive and efficient methods of cultivation than those traditionally practiced. This shift corresponds to the emergence of the magisterial gaze as an encoding of the increasing land mastery and settlement.

This is brought home in the discussion of Plate XV, *View from Fishkill, Looking to West-Point,* where the author speculates on the area's potential:

There is still in the recesses, as well as on the summits of the mountains, a wide field for the industry and enterprise of the pioneer; although it may excite some surprise, that immediately on the verge of a noble stream, communicating with the most populous and commercial city of the Union, such extensive tracts of land should be found, which have never known the touch of the plough-

30

Fig. 6. William G. Wall,
Little Falls at Luzerne, 1828.
Reproduced in *Hudson River
Port Folio* (New York: Henry I.
Megarey), Plate I.

Fig. 7. William G. Wall, *The Junction of the Sacandaga and Hudson Rivers*, 1828, Plate II.

share. . . . There can be no doubt, however, that every day will tend to diminish this cause of enterprise traversing this great State. . . . Here has been literally illustrated by the metaphorical language of the Holy Writ: Here is a voice in the wilderness—here the crooked places have been made straight, and the rough places plain; the valleys exalted, and the mountains levelled: here, as with the rod of Moses, the rock which has been stricken has poured forth waters in the desert; and where loneliness and sterility reigned, are now to be found the blessings of a fertile soil and an opulent population.

The mythical formulation of American futurity is already being encoded textually as the magisterial gaze and justified with biblical prophecy, as if American expansion had been foreordained by the Godhead. The allusion to Moses would later be incorporated pictorially in landscape motifs where the Hebrew leader is seen gazing from a distant summit upon the Promised Land.

Unfortunately, the promised land in both biblical and real time was already populated by indigenous peoples who had to be displaced to make room for the new settlers. Wall wants to diminish and even completely bury this history in the construction of his myth, as is strikingly evident in his description of *Rapids near Hadley's Falls* (Plate IV): "If this section of the country was, at any time, memorable as the scene of conflict, its celebrity has long since passed away for want of a record to perpetuate it. It is more than probable, however, that no event of an important character, *no circumstance exceeding the limited and transient interest of perhaps an Indian broil, has occurred in the neighborhood of these falls*" (emphasis added). Similarly, when considering the historical site of *Fort Edward* (Plate X), Wall is quick to embed the conflict between indigenous peoples and their invaders in a historical process that not only eliminates guilt but also elevates the latter at the expense of the former: "The ploughshare now peacefully turns up the soil moistened by the blood of thousands: the dust of the merciless Indian and the ambitious European repose in awful amity together; the echoes of the woods have slept long, since they responded to the harsh discords of war: but the memory of days of glorious enterprise remains vigorous as at first, and the scene of their operation will be held sacred to the remotest ages."

Thus every component of the myth is set into place, needing only a visual encoding to complete the picture. Indeed, in Plate XI, *Troy from Mount Ida,* we begin to catch a glimpse of this unfolding process in Wall's seminal album. As the author declares:

Perhaps, in the annals of the United States, there is scarcely to be found an instance of more rapid growth, than in the case of Troy. This city was first laid out in lots in 1787; and, in the course of five years, from a farm, it presented the appearance of a respectable and flourishing place. The amazing change which

has been subsequently wrought, is almost as much to be attributed to the industry and enterprise of its inhabitants, who came from the eastern states, as to the inimitable advantages of its situation. Its population is now supposed to be upward of four thousand souls, and the trade which it commands with the northern and western districts of the State, as well as with the metropolis, gives the assurance of future increase at least in an equal proportion.

The illustration accompanying this text depicts the town on the east shore of the Hudson as seen from Mount Ida just beyond Troy, from whose summit "the eye embraces a most extensive and enchanting view" (Fig. 8). The projection of a thriving city newly carved out of the wilderness from the summit of a nearby hill is consistent with the mature formulation of the magisterial gaze, demonstrated in the representation. Here text and image are bonded into a coded unity, unlike the majority of the other illustrations concerned with power rela-

34

Fig. 8. William G. Wall, *Troy from Mount Ida*, 1828. Reproduced in *Hudson River Port Folio* (New York: Henry I. Megarey), Plate XI.

tions expressed through property. By 1840, the illustrations of such albums will be predominantly organized around the azimuth of the magisterial gaze.

Scholars of American art history continue to debate the loosely used label "Hudson River school" as well as the even more elusive "luminist" tag attached to some nineteenth-century landscapists.[44] While acknowledging distinctions of light, technique, and compositional strategies in individual cases, I believe these differences, however, are less significant than the central, underlying component that the Hudson River and luminist artists all share and that unites them across generations: the desire to carve out unity, harmony, and order from endless vistas. The preoccupation with light, the surface treatment, atmospheric effects, and use of baroque conventions may vary from artist to artist, group to group, but the assumed presence of the spectator, the hori-

zontal format, the directional sense of gradual descent from a height to the valley and generally—with the exception of Martin Johnson Heade and Fitz Hugh Lane—from overgrown thicket to clearing or body of water to the trappings of civilization, are central to every landscapist grouped at one time or another under the Hudson River or luminist rubrics.

The early and late works of the so-called luminists John F. Kensett and Sanford R. Gifford[45] contain striking examples of the application of the magisterial gaze, displaying the amplitude of space and extensive prospect common to Cole, Durand, Church, and Bierstadt (Figs. 9, 10). It is true that in many of the pictures by Heade, Fitz Hugh Lane, and Kensett the standard wilderness coulisse or framing device at the lateral edges of Cole and Durand is absent, and the appearance of an uncluttered horizon mitigates against the focused

Fig. 9. John Frederick Kensett, *Hudson River Scene*, 1857. The Metropolitan Museum of Art, New York. Gift of H. D. Babcock in memory of S. D. Babcock, 1907.

Fig. 10. John Frederick Kensett, *Autumn Afternoon on Lake George.* In the collection of the Corcoran Gallery of Art, Museum Purchase, Gallery Fund, Washington, D.C.

gaze. But most often there are strategically located objects in the foreground proscenium or middle-ground water that subtly guide the eye to a single point of emphasis. And although the absence of the framing device eliminates a clue to the precise position of the artist and conceals the transition from the heights to the depths, no one could deny that the panorama is being viewed from the heights or that the horizontal expanses constitute the primary aim of the luminist pictures.

The magisterial gaze embodied the exaltation of a cultured American elite before the illimitable horizon that they identified with the destiny of the American nation.[46] Its appearance coincides with the era of hopefulness following the end of the War of 1812, the expression of the sense of enormous possibility that Americans were beginning to share about the future of their new country and their desire to root out vestiges of the Old World. This expression is most vividly dramatized in Cooper's *The Pioneers,* first published in 1823.[47] The real estate of Judge Temple is subsumed under the metaphor of the landscape viewed from the summit, construed as the panorama of an individual's control over civilization-culture. The way into it is fraught with danger, both in terms of the precipitous cliffs that confront the climber at every turn and the Native Americans who have been removed to make way for the new culture. But in the end the march of progress beckons to a higher realm of experience.

Judge Temple, who has named the summit of his mountain Mount Vision, recounts the initial discovery of the spectacular view of the valley that seemed to him "as the deceptions of a dream." He had an unextended view of the wilderness where there was as yet no sign of human life. This would soon change, however, for the mind of Temple was disposed "to look far into futurity, in his speculations on the improvements that posterity were to make in his lands. To his eye, where others saw nothing but a wilderness, towns, manufactories, bridges, canals, mines, and all the other resources of an old country were constantly presenting themselves." When the judge's daughter, Elizabeth, expresses astonishment at the sheriff's projection of the town's expansion into a marshland zone, the sheriff replies, "We must run our streets by the compass . . . and disregard trees, hills, ponds, stumps, or, in fact, any thing but posterity. Such is the will of your father." And Elizabeth, now with full understanding, exclaims, "The enterprise of Judge Temple is taming the very forests!"[48] Then, taking it out of the realm of the personal, she adds, "How rapidly is civilization treading on the footsteps of nature!"

The dislocation of the Native American population, represented in the novel by John Mohegan, wounds Elizabeth's sensibilities, for she believes that he has prior claim to the land now owned by her father. But she accepts the inevitability of "progress": "What can I do? What can my father do?" She reasons that if they offered John a home his innate disposition would compel him to refuse them, and they are not "so silly as to wish such a thing, could we convert these clearings and farms, again, into hunting-grounds, as the Leather-stocking would wish to see them!"[49]

Judge Temple's transformation of the mountain view is irreversible and inevitable, and weak consciences and anachronistic lifestyles must give way to the brute fact of his "activity and enterprise." For all his picturesque descriptions of the landscape, Cooper is intent in the novel to establish its geographical and topographical fact. The land owned by the judge lies in the valley of the Otsego, "east of a meridional line drawn through the center of the state." The entire first chapter is devoted to the topographic setting, a fertile, arable region fed by the sources of the Susquehanna River, which unite to "form one of the proudest rivers of the United States." Beautiful and thriving villages are interspersed among the margins of the small lakes or situated at those points of the streams favorable to manufacturing, "and neat and comfortable farms, with every indication of wealth about them, are scattered profusely through the vales, and even to the mountain tops." The newcomer also encounters academies and "minor edifices of learning," attesting to the cultural advance of the community, and places of worship "abound with that frequency which characterizes a moral and reflecting people, and with that variety of exterior and canonical government which flows from unfettered liberty of conscience." The entire region demonstrates what a people can accomplish in rugged wilderness "under the dominion of mild laws, and where every man feels a direct interest in the prosperity of a commonwealth, of which he knows himself to form a part."[50]

The view from the summit manifests the material traces of the development of this history. From the remnant of the forest with its abandoned pioneer cabin and Indian burial site, the eye wanders to the clearing in the vale and the commencement of agriculture. The stubs of trees stripped of their bark abounded in the open fields adjacent to the village, but what might have been an "unpleasant" aspect of the view went unseen from the mountain, where Elizabeth could see "only in gross the cluster of houses that lay like a map at her feet." This transition state makes a vivid impression on Judge Temple and the young hero of the novel, despite their greater familiarity with it:

> Five years had wrought greater changes than a century would produce in countries where time and labor have given permanency to the works of man. To the young hunter and the Judge

the scene had less of novelty; though none ever emerge from the dark forests of the mountain, and witness the glorious scenery of that beauteous valley, as it burst unexpectedly upon them, without a feeling of delight. The former cast one admiring glance from north to south, had sunk his face again beneath the folds of his coat; while the latter contemplated, with philanthropic pleasure, the prospect of affluence and comfort, that was expanding around him; the result of his own enterprise, and much of it the fruits of his own industry.[51]

This is the view of the author himself, who exerted a powerful influence on the imaginative thought of American writers and artists of the next generation. Judge Temple was modeled after Cooper's father, who owned extensive wilderness tracts, and the initial sight from the summit described by the fictional character was based on his father's personal recollection. Indeed, General James Clinton led expeditions against the Indians in the mid-

1780s in support of settlement in the region and sent a team of surveyors to map it. Cooper's father, who apparently had bought the lands unseen years before on speculation, formed part of the surveying team, exactly as did his fictional persona, who momentarily separated from the survey party "and rode to the summit of the mountain that I have since called Mount Vision."[52] It was with a view to people the land that Temple joined the survey expedition, land that had been confiscated from the Tories and that he had purchased at low prices. The picturesque valley of the Otsego had a particularly violent history, but Temple's success effaced the past and beckoned to the future.

In his preface, Cooper boasts that "Otsego has now become one of the most populous districts of New York. It sends forth its emigrants like any other old region; and it is pregnant with industry and enterprise." The key to Cooper's theme is this statement, related to the

by now familiar story of the westward movement. Its importance is underscored by his
concluding passage on Leather-stocking, forced
to retreat to the wilderness as the result of the
transformation of the land: "He had gone far
towards the setting sun,—the foremost in that
band of Pioneers, who are opening the way for
the march of the nation across the continent."
Despite Cooper's sympathy for the dispossessed
John Mohegan and Natty Bumpo, both of
whom need the wilderness to survive, he
stresses the nature of an irreversible process,
which he finally accepts wholeheartedly.

Bumpo is unaware of this process, the pioneer who paves the way for the yeoman. He
himself expresses the dominant thought as it is
metaphorically embodied in the mountain
summit. Bumpo's other favorite paradise was
the range of Catskills in New York where he
hunted on High-Peak and the Round-top and
from where one could see "Creation, all

creation." From the flat on the top of that
mountain, Bumpo "often found the place
where Albany stands." Cooper picks up his
main thesis in his novel *The Prairie,* published
four years later, in which Leather-stocking has
moved to "that portion of the American Union
which lies between the Alleghenies and the
Rockies." Cooper lauds the Louisiana Purchase,
which "gave us the sole command of the great
thoroughfare of the interior, and placed the
countless tribes of savages, who lay along our
borders, entirely within our control." The
graduations of society, from refined to "barbar-
ity," related to the march of progress, "ever-
receding borders which mark the skirts and an-
nounce the approach of the nation, as moving
mists precede the signs of the day." Significantly, Leather-stocking dies without heirs and
states near the end, "When I am gone, there
will be an end to my race." He insists on being
buried "beyond the din of the settlements," yet

in his last moments "his gaze seemed fastened on the clouds which hung around the western horizon, reflecting the bright colors, and giving form and loveliness to the glorious tints of an American sunset." Unknowingly, Leatherstocking made it possible for the settlements, which he professes to despise, to grow and thus pave the way for the glorious future of the nation.

Although *The Prairie* is set in the plains, it is the view from the summits of the Alleghenies and, subsequently, the view from the peaks of the Rockies that exemplify the ethos behind the westward expansion. The novel is actually an extension of *The Pioneers,* beginning where the other leaves off. Henceforth all literary and aesthetic visions of the westward expansion will take the form of this summit view, the magisterial gaze perhaps receiving its most self-conscious formulation in Emanuel Leutze's *Westward the Course of Empire Takes Its*

Way, which, not fortuitously, is located on the west wall of the Capitol (Fig. 11).[53] Contracted between Leutze and Captain Montgomery C. Meigs (then in charge of the additions to the Capitol) in 1861, it takes as its theme a line from an eighteenth-century poem ("Verses on the Prospect of Planting Arts and Learning in America") by Bishop George Berkeley that had been recast by Eugene Lies as "Westward, Ho!" in *The United States Magazine, and Democratic Review* in 1849. Like the mural it inspired (Leutze's original title was *Westward Ho!*), it is a paean to Manifest Destiny:

> Westward, ho! since first the sun
> Over young creation shone,
>   Westward has the light progressed.
> Westward arts and creeds have tended,
> Never shall their march be ended,
>   Till they reach the utmost West.
>
> . . . .

44

Fig. 11. Emanuel Leutze,
*Westward the Course of Empire
Takes Its Way.* 1862. United
States Capitol Art Collection,
Washington, D.C.

Is it that all earthly things
Westward ply their restless wings,
　　Problems of their being to solve?
Faith and Knowledge, Commerce, Wealth,
Valor, Strength and manly Health
　　Do they, like the stars, revolve?

. . . .

Europe's noon hath long been past;
All her vain insignia cast
　　Lengthening shadows on her brow;
Soon she'll mourn, in darkness shrouded,
For her blue sky, dimly clouded,
　　Ev'n as Asia mourneth now.

Westward, ho! the morning breaks;
Lo! a younger world awakes;
　　There the day-god long shall rest;
Nor can wild Hesperian dreams,
Dreams of golden earth and steams,
　　Lure him to a further west.[54]

Leutze's monumental fresco shows the irrepressible thrust of the pioneers, who pause momentarily to savor their triumph as they crest the Continental Divide. They stand heroically at the pinnacle of the Rockies—the most elevated of them prepares to raise the Stars and Stripes à la Frémont—gesturing in the direction of the vast spaces beyond. Leutze's philosophical justification for the forward thrust of empire is inscribed in the right-hand border, ornamented with a medallion of Daniel Boone: "The spirit grows with its allotted spaces. The Mind is narrowed in a narrow Sphere." But whose mind and whose spirit? Encoded in this representation of the magisterial gaze are the sexism (the outsized frontiersman with the coonskin cap embracing his diminutive, swooning wife and daughter) and the racism (the absence of the Native American and the location of the lone black figure, a teamster, below the peak and

46

Fig. 12. Anonymous, *"Westward the Course of Empire Takes Its Way" with McCormick Reapers in the Van*, lithograph, undated. Chicago Historical Society, Chicago.

unable to share in the vision) that are intimately related to the American striving for national conquest.

We know what lay in the vision of those hardy pioneers through a parody of the composition used as an ad for McCormick Reapers (Fig. 12).[55] The popular chromolithograph of the late 1860s or early 1870s, *"Westward the Course of Empire Takes Its Way" with McCormick Reapers in the Van,* spells out what the pioneers see in the promised land. Instead of a vast wilderness, they behold a scene of immense farms where a legion of farmers running McCormick reapers are busily at work harvesting grain. On the distant horizon they see thriving towns punctuated by tall chimneys releasing their smoke into the air. Here the potential signified by the magisterial gaze is satisfied with a vengeance.

The western expansion and the romantic ideology that accompanied it and conveyed it to the public were products of an Eastern consciousness sensitized to the view from the heights. Just as America was the product of a European colonizing tradition, so the West was the product of an Eastern mercantile mind-set. The general who commanded the expedition into the lands owned by James Fenimore Cooper's father was himself the father of DeWitt Clinton, governor of New York in the 1820s and the most vociferous promoter of the Erie Canal, which opened in 1825. Clinton had conceived of the daring idea of digging the "big ditch" and carried it through to success. The Erie Canal did for upper New York State what the later Western railroads did for the plains states. When it officially opened, most of the 363 miles it covered were still wilderness, but it did not take long for the hordes of settlers and speculators to find their way along its towpaths, woodlands, and fertile river valleys, and its terminus at the mouth of the

Hudson became a national focus, surpassing for a time Boston, Philadelphia, and New Orleans as the country's chief seaport. Boomtowns sprang up across the new frontier as the canal facilitated the transportation of people and products into the wilderness areas.[56]

The opening of the canal coincided with the foundation of the Hudson River school, whose patrons included Clinton and Cooper. Its success in fact depended on the national importance of New York following the opening of the canal and the emphasis on the Hudson River as the primary water route between the East Coast and the Middle West. The reigning elite wished to record and celebrate the untapped wilderness, the resumption of cultural and commercial ties with England, its own growing power within metropolitan New York City. Besides being an adroit businessman and administrator, Clinton was one of the most active promoters of the American Academy of the Fine Arts, forerunner of the National Academy of Design. Clinton addressed the crowd at the inauguration of the American Academy in 1816, stressing the need for American artists to capture nature's "operations on a magnificent scale" in their own country and the need for society to support them in this endeavor.

The acknowledged founder of the new school, Thomas Cole, made his debut in New York the year the canal opened. He was singled out by Philip Hone, the mayor of New York and one of the city's wealthiest collectors. A close friend of Clinton's and fellow promoter of the Erie Canal, Hone purchased two views by Cole of the Hudson River. The relation between the canal and landscape painting was made in an address delivered before the American Academy on 17 November 1825 by Richard Ray. Ray extolled the growing role of arts in American culture, pointing to a stage of development "when the division of property gives to a favored class the choice of amusement and relaxations of leisure." In this development, the

landscapist is especially fortunate: "For him extends the unappropriated world, where the
glance of genius may descry new combinations
of colors, and new varieties of prospect." There
in desolate scenes of "cascades of deep glens,
and darkly shaded caverns,"

> he may plant the brown Indian, with feathered
> crest and bloody tomahawk, the picturesque
> and native offspring of the wilderness. Come
> then, son of art, the genius of your country
> points you to its stupendous cataracts, its
> highlands intersected with the majestic river,
> its ranging mountains, its softer and enchant-
> ing scenery. There, where Nature needs no fic-
> titious charms, where the eye requires no bor-
> rowed assistance from the memory, place on
> the canvass the lovely landscape and adorn our
> houses with American prospects and American
> skies.[57]

When Ray uses the term "American prospects," we now know what he implies; and the
planting of the "brown Indian" is exactly that:

a self-conscious symbolization of a passing
order to complement the promising prospects.
The term "prospects," like "horizons," carries
with it the double meaning of future opportu-
nities and enchanting views, the sense of the
physical landscape as the site for wealth and
position. Cooper took his father as his ideal, an
enterprising gentry for whom future prospects
and landscape prospects were synonymous. And
it is Cole, deeply influenced by Cooper, and his
disciple Asher B. Durand (who did the frontis-
piece for Ray's published version of his address)
who put together an aesthetic system appropriate to the ideology of expansion in upper New
York State. In 1829 Cole joined the throngs of
travelers up the canal and in his journal praised
the wonders of commerce and industry along
the artificial waterway.

Cole's painting systematically begins from
a mountain height or hill and looks down on a
valley pierced by the Hudson River (Fig. 13).
Typically, the peaceful view of the valley, with

Fig. 13. Thomas Cole, *Sunny Morning on the Hudson River*, ca. 1827. Gift of Martha C. Karolik for the M. and M. Karolik Collection of American Paintings, 1815–1865, Courtesy, Museum of Fine Arts, Boston.

its signs of settlement and human activity, is contrasted with a rugged foreground zone marked by a singular blasted tree. In this instance, Cole also added a disused Indian altar, thus signifying the vanishing breed in the face of the changing landscape prospect. More familiar is Cole's *Oxbow* (*The Connecticut River near Northampton*), painted in 1836 and viewed from the top of Mount Holyoke (Fig. 14). Holyoke was one of the first of the mountaintops to be frequented by tourists; a hut to accommodate travelers was erected there as early as 1821.[58] As in the previous work, Cole organizes the main axis of the composition along a diagonal line of sight starting from the left foreground and culminating in the right middle ground. Cole again deploys the left foreground in a *repoussoir* fashion, standing for the wilderness past with its desolate blasted trees, while beyond this darkened zone lies the sun-filled valley of the Connecticut River with its fertile meadows and terraced fields leading "to one of the most sunny and cheerful villages in Massachusetts."[59]

Nathaniel Parker Willis and others always reminded the reader that the history of Mount Holyoke and the region along the river was marked by events of Indian warfare. Homes of white settlers were burned and the inhabitants killed or taken captive. The early settlers bravely defended themselves against the "aggressions" of the populous Indian tribes. Eventually this land was purchased from the rascally savages; one tract of ninety square miles was traded for a hundred fathoms of wampum and ten coats—quite a bargain for nearly five thousand acres. Like today's Los Angeles real estate broker, Willis cannot resist letting the reader know that at the time of his writing the land was worth eight hundred thousand to nine hundred thousand dollars. He adds as an uneasy footnote that "unjust as the transaction

52

Fig. 14. Thomas Cole, *Oxbow (The Connecticut River near Northampton)*, 1836. The Metropolitan Museum of Art, New York. Gift of Mrs. Russell Sage, 1908. (See color plate.)

seems, however, the prize was ample to the Indian who could not have got so much by keeping it, and for whom there was no other purchaser."[60] This is Yankee double-talk, and it assumes that the Indians wanted to sell their lands desperately at that moment.

I will return to Willis later, but for now I want to emphasize the association of Cole's landscape with the dispossession of hereditary Indian land, its transformation into property, and the visual projection of this metamorphosed land in the view from the summit. It may be recalled that in his "Essay on American Scenery," Cole contemplated the futurity of the nation from an imaginary height: "Where the wolf roams, the plough shall glisten; on the gray crag shall rise temple and tower—mighty deeds shall be done in the now pathless wilderness." Here is his textual delineation of his graphic rendition of the idea of futurity and the overcoming of the human and material obstacles to this progress. It is this challenge to the Euro-Americans that makes the civilizing process so basic to their idea of advance—carried out with the sense of a God-ordained mission.[61] Cole rendered the country seat of his Connecticut patron Daniel Wadsworth as viewed from the topmost peak on the vast estate, marking it as a salient stage in the cultivation of the wilderness as the mansion looks out on the settlement of Farmington farther down in the Farmington and Connecticut river valleys (Fig. 15).[62] Cole isolates the magnificent country mansion with brilliant sunlight, a sparkling jewel of civilization in contrast with the blasted tree of the wilderness above. The progressive descent is a metaphor for the progression of culture under divine sanction, and Wadsworth had this in mind when he named his estate Monte Video—"I see the mountain." Cole's identification with this perspective is seen in his obsession with the summit view: two years before he painted Wadsworth's picture he made a difficult ascent to a mountain

54

Fig. 15. Thomas Cole, *View of Monte Video, the Seat of Daniel Wadsworth, Esq.*, 1828. Wadsworth Atheneum, Hartford. Bequest of Daniel Wadsworth.

peak in the Catskills with "a wide prospect," and clambering up to the bare rocks jutting out he took a seat "upon my mountain throne, the monarch of the scene."[63] Later, he constructed a workshop-home in the Catskills "in the Italian Villa style," which "commanded" a spectacular view of the valley.[64]

When seen in the context of that impulsion, the despoiling of nature could only have taken a secondary place in the thought of Cole and his elite patrons. When it came down to a choice between an unencumbered prospect or forest preservation, Cole chose the former. Once when he climbed a hill with Durand to get a view, he was disappointed to find that a mass of wood "hid the anticipated prospect. For once I wished the axe had not been stayed."[65] Willis articulated this contradiction most emphatically in his *American Scenery:*

> The picturesque views of the United States suggest a train of thought directly opposite to that of similar objects of interest in other lands. There the soul and centre of attraction in every picture is some ruin of the past. . . . The objects and habits of reflection in both traveller and artist undergo in America a direct revolution. He who journeys here, if he would not have the eternal succession of lovely natural objects—"Lie like a load on the weary eye," must feed his imagination on the future. The American does so. His mind, as he tracks the broad rivers of his own country, is perpetually reaching forward. Instead of looking through a valley, which has presented the same aspect for hundreds of years—in which live lords and tenants, whose hearths have been surrounded by the same names through ages of tranquil descent, and whose fields have never changed landmark or mode of culture since the memory of man, he sees a valley laden down like a harvest waggon with a virgin vegetation, untrodden and luxuriant; and his first thought is of the villages that will soon sparkle on the hillsides, the axes that will ring from the woodlands, and the mills, bridges, canals, and railroads, that will span and border the stream

that now runs through sedge and wild-flowers. The towns he passes through on his route are not recognizable by prints done by artists long ago dead, with houses of low-browed architecture, and immemorial trees; but a town which has perhaps doubled its inhabitants and dwellings since he last saw it, and will again double them before he returns. Instead of inquiring into its antiquity, he sits over the fire with his paper and pencil, and calculates what the population will be in ten years, how far they will spread, what the value of the neighboring land will become, and whether the stock of some canal or railroad that seems more visionary than Symmes's expedition to the centre of the earth, will, in consequence, be a good investment. He looks upon all external objects as exponents of the future.[66]

Here in one grand nutshell is the landscape ideology of the dominant elite of the Eastern Seaboard in the pre–Civil War era and the mainspring of the westward movement.

And it is wholly unsurprising that almost all of Willis's vignettes are based on views from an elevated site, exemplified in the engraved illustrations by William Henry Bartlett. He gazes upon Boston from Dorchester Heights, a view he describes as "very commanding." This leads him to contemplate the investment property below: "The calenture of speculation is just now at its height in America; and Dorchester, like other places, is laid out in lots, and busy with the builders of fancy cottages and hotels. If calculation has not overreached itself, the suburbs of Boston will soon sparkle with villas on every hillside within the horizon."[67] Thus is American scenery for sale. Gazing upon Lake George near the town of Caldwell, he was presented "with a prospect superior to any which I ever beheld." But the scenery stood incomplete, for

the efforts of cultivation are obviously wanting. The hand of the husbandman has already begun to clear these grounds, and will, at no great distance of time, adorn them with all the smiling scenes of agriculture. It does not demand the gift of prophecy to foresee, that the villas of opulence and refinement will, within half a century, add here all the elegances of art to the beauty and majesty of nature.[68]

Standing on the platform of the famous Mountain-House in the Catskills, he ruminates,

> From the Mountain-House, the busy and all-glorious Hudson is seen winding half its silver length—towns, villas, and white spires, sparkling on the shores, and snowy sails and gaily-painted steamers specking its bosom. It is a constant diorama of the most lively beauty; and the traveller, as he looks down upon it, sighs to make it a home.[69]

A passing twinge of guilt grips him at one point on Jefferson's Rock, overlooking the valley of the Shenandoah: "It is difficult, at least for me, to stand on any eminence commanding a landscape, wild, yet formed for a blest human residence, without seeing in it the forfeited inheritance of the red man."[70] Although moments later he convinces himself that Native Americans were doomed to extinction in any event, what is important about this frank admission is the evidence that the literary and visual trope of the summit view and its associations with past and future of the American dream had already become deeply ingrained within the American imagination. The progressive descent into an ever-widening vista is a revelation of God's reward in the vastness of an ever-expanding cultivation.

Cole's brilliant disciple, Frederic Edwin Church, assimilated that outlook in both his work and personal life. One of his earliest works, *Moses Viewing the Promised Land* (1846), gives the formula a biblical twist by locating the Hebrew leader on a table rock looking out

Fig. 16. Frederic Edwin
Church, *Mount Ktaadn*, 1853.
Yale University Art Gallery,
New Haven. Stanley B. Resor,
B.A. 1901, Fund. (See color
plate.)

over the verdant vales of a promised, and promising, land. (He would later return to this theme in *Jerusalem from the Mount of Olives*, showing a radiant and visionary biblical metropolis from a distant hilltop perspective.) His desire to bring his landscape in line with the national destiny is perhaps most strikingly revealed in his *Mount Ktaadn* (the same peak in the Katahdin region of Maine that attracted Thoreau), projecting an extensive prospect across a valley culminating with the mountain on the far-flung horizon (Fig. 16). An adolescent male on the upper level sits meditatively beneath a tree and gazes downhill across a stream to a manufactory, probably a textile mill, in the middle distance. The location signifies a stage of development in the infinitely expanding prospect of the youth and, by inference, of the young American nation.[71] The owner of this work was Marshall O. Roberts, a shrewd New York steamship and railroad investor who used his insider's information to buy up undeveloped areas along newly planned routes.

Even when Church renders a desolate wilderness scene, absent of all human presence, the magisterial gaze is there to shape and organize it into a work fit for American consumption. The irony of *Twilight in the Wilderness* is that it still reflects Church's notion that America was vast beyond exhaustion, a place of unlimited horizons. The invisible onlooker commands these wilderness lands as surely as the mill owner in *Mount Ktaadn*.[72] The view faces into the setting sun, a westward orientation signifying that the urge to expansion makes this tract of wilderness a passing scene. Not surprisingly, the work was painted for the railway baron William T. Walters of Baltimore, whose vast landholdings demonstrated that he was more than happy to resign himself to the inevitable.

Church's first major success, *Niagara*

(1857), represented a spectacular variation on the theme of the magisterial gaze. From a point just above Table Rock overlooking Horseshoe Falls on the Canadian side, the spectator could command a vast, receding space shot through with the violent energy of cascading waters.[73] The futurity of American empire is metaphorically actualized on the horizon as unlimited and unconstrained power. The picturing of the harnessing and unleashing of colossal forces in the drive westward required a natural analogy on the order and magnitude of Niagara. One writer observed that the stimulus of the "terrible" Niagara on art inevitably related to the national outlook. Art born of this inspiration is the

> result of democracy, of individuality, of the expansion of each, of the liberty allowed to all. . . . It is inspired not only by the irresistible cataract, but by the mighty forest, by the thousand miles of river, by the broad continent we call our own, by the onward march of civilization, by the conquering of savage areas; characteristic alike of the western backwoodsman, of the Arctic explorer, the southern filibuster, and the northern merchant.[74]

G. W. Curtis described the falls in 1855 as an American symbol of "irresistible progress" and imagined their roar as an inspirational voice urging the nation onward with the loud stentorian note: "FORWARD!"[75] The symbolic use of the torrential currents to suggest the demoniacal in expansionism is seen in Melville's *Moby Dick*. In the chapter entitled "Sunset" (that is, facing west), Ahab applies a railroad analogy to his frenzied maritime quest for the White Whale: "The path to my fixed purpose is laid with iron rails, whereon my soul is grooved to run. Over unsounded gorges, through the rifled hearts of mountains, under torrents' beds, unerringly I rush! Naught's an obstacle, naught's an angle to the iron way!"

That onlookers of Niagara experienced a rush of power from their managerial view had become something of a cliché by Church's time, but listen to a comment by a visitor in 1815: "The whole power of the world seemed insufficient to prevent our unrestrained and almost libertine indulgence in the magnificent scene. I was almost tempted to wish that there still might exist some doubt of our reaching it. It seemed to detract from the power of nature that the Falls should be so completely at our command, so entirely abased at our feet."[76]

Church's monumental South American scenes, starting with the *Heart of the Andes* (1859), deal with a foreign terrain and so convey a more ambiguous message. Nevertheless, his attempt to condense into one colossal, compositelike panorama the geological, meteorological, and botanical history of South America is analogous to the historical synchronicity of the magisterial gaze.[77] The stupefying view

ranges far above the tops of the trees, traversing a village in the middle distance and moving into the immense distance beyond.[78] Church first traveled to South America in 1853 with Cyrus W. Field to explore its commercial possibilities, and in such a case the magisterial gaze would have been converted into the more conditional "entrepreneurial gaze." It may be recalled that five years later Field orchestrated the successful laying of the first transatlantic cable, thus establishing a line of communication between continents.[79] In the same way, Church's scenes of Colombia and Ecuador, coinciding with a period of intensive U.S. exploration of Spanish America in the wake of the Mexican War, may be understood as southern extensions of the magisterial gaze.[80] (In one telling incident on his trip, Church ordered his peons to cut a swath through jungle grass to give him an unencumbered view of the horizon.[81])

Cyrus Field, a competitively ambitious minister's son who infused his social and political ideology with old-time religion, has never been deemed worthy of Church's company in the art historical literature. But it was Field who financed the expedition to South America and invited Church to join it. Field should be regarded as no less than Church's patron, for whom the painter executed several pictures, including an early view of Cotopaxi, the grand volcanic mass in the Ecuadoran Andes that fascinated Church for nearly fifteen years. Field was close friends with men like the historian George Bancroft, a visionary spokesman for the emerging concept of America's Manifest Destiny, and the railroad and steamship magnate Marshall O. Roberts, who was obsessed with the idea of the nation's infinite expansion.[82] Roberts owned several works by the painter, including *Mount Ktaadn,* again attesting to his tight-knit relations with Field and his circle of prominent advocates for America's Manifest Destiny.

Church's acquaintance with Field antedated his first trip to South America and in fact dates from his youth. Field began his career as a merchant. After working for the dry goods merchant and department store pioneer Alexander T. Stewart, Field left in 1838 to join his brother's paper manufactory in Lee, Massachusetts, where he worked as a sales representative. There he became acquainted with other New England papermaking families, including the Churches. Church's father, Joseph, was then connected with the family firm, one of the first mills in Lee, where Frederic spent a good deal of his time sketching.[83] Although Frederic was younger than Field, they struck up a close friendship, and the two often took Sunday walks around the countryside. Field commissioned the precocious Church to go to Madison, Connecticut, to depict his grandfather's home—one of the neglected works of the painter's legacy at Olana on the Hudson.[84]

In the early 1840s Field opened his own paper business in New York City and specialized in tinted papers with fanciful names like "peach" and "salmon" or ranged them in an order reminiscent of the painter's palette: super blue, superfine blue, and extra super blue. The burgeoning of the news media and the general expansion of business sent the paper business soaring, and by 1847 Field and Company could boast a remarkable gross sales total of $354,432.60. His commercial success allowed him to begin a collection of paintings from the Hudson River school, a move that no doubt signals the influence of Church, who in 1844 had moved to the Catskills to study with Thomas Cole.

Field's concern with European competition led him to travel extensively in England and on the Continent in search of the materials and

tools of foreign manufacture that would give his products the look of imports. By midcentury, when Field was only thirty, his firm stood as one of the largest wholesale paper firms in New York. During those years, Field and Church maintained their close friendship, and Church frequently visited him at his New York City home. In 1851 Church proposed to Field and his wife that they tour some of the key natural wonders of the country, and in June all three traveled by train to Virginia and Kentucky and explored by steamboat the upper Mississippi River region, completing their trip together at St. Paul in the newly formed Minnesota Territory. At that point, Church abruptly left the party to hurry east to do studies for his projected painting of Niagara Falls.

Thus Church's engagement with what he perceived to be the paradigmatic natural metaphor for the national potential was preceded by his western trek in the company of the Fields and his search for analogous symbolic sites. Indeed, it was during this trip that Field commissioned the picture *Natural Bridge, Virginia,* which Church completed the following year. Cyrus monitored the sketching sessions and was so anxious that Church render the site with photographic accuracy that he climbed the limestone cliffs to collect rock specimens to guide Church's conception. Church rejected such props, but Field held on to them to check the painter's definitive work against the samples. Field promised to pay for the painting only on condition that they matched, which they did.

Field's demands tell us a good deal about the dependence of the artist on the patron and suggest their common outlook. They may have differed as to means, but their ends were similar. When Field learned at St. Paul that the Sioux tribes along the Minnesota River were ready to sign away a large portion of their lands to white people in return for muskets and ammunition, he immediately chartered a steamboat to watch the spectacle. Field was amused that the arrival of the party and the shrill noise of the whistle frightened the Native Americans, halting the negotiations until the boat could be removed out of sight. Field's response represented the stereotyped attitude expressed in popular illustration in which Native Americans appear distressed at the sight of the white man's technology. He then wrote about his experience to Church, who shared Field's excitement over the treaty and whose reply characterized the event as one of "extraordinary interest."[85]

On their return to New York Cyrus and Mary Field moved into a luxurious house in Gramercy Park. Field was now listed among the thirty-three richest people in the city (gross sales in 1852 totaled $812,267.82). His opulent mansion was hung with landscapes from the Hudson River school, a number of which had been painted by Church, including the remarkable *West Rock, New Haven,* one of the most famous scenic views in the neighborhood of New Haven. Although the middleground is dominated by the dome-shaped rock, a striking geological formation, the landscape was viewed from a high altitude that sets the motif into a spacious panoramic format. Field and Church had a common interest in geological processes, with Field's comprehensive collection of fossils and minerals distinctly attesting to his mining interests. Church pictured for Field the large-scale possibilities of science, and in turn Field's taste for Hudson River scenes complemented his growing material control and expansionist interests.

Late in 1852 Field came across an epistolary series of articles by Matthew Fontaine Maury in the *National Intelligencer* entitled

"The Amazon and the Atlantic Slope of South America."[86] Sorely neglected today, Maury was a maritime geographer, astronomer, meteorologist, and prominent government advocate of scientific involvement in the process of Manifest Destiny. He placed the fields of oceanography and agricultural meteorology on a systematic footing to abet economic expansion, and his investigations made possible the laying of the Atlantic cable. He used his position as superintendent of the Naval Observatory to broadcast scientific cooperation between nations and unrestricted trade practices. He enjoyed great prestige in the international scientific community (although less so at home) and established close relations with such noted scientists as Yale geologist Benjamin Silliman and the Prussian naturalist Alexander von Humboldt—both influential in the thought of Field and Church.[87]

In 1851 Maury—a naval officer sidelined

because of a physical injury—persuaded the Secretary of the Navy to send a two-man expedition to reconnoiter the Amazon from the Andes to its mouth, and it was on their observations that he based his series. Published between 17 November and 3 December 1852, Maury's articles in the *National Intelligencer* emphasized the mineral and agricultural potential of this rich but as yet undeveloped area. Although Maury signed the articles "Inca," the author's real identity was hardly a secret. Earlier in the year, in connection with a railroad convention in New Orleans, Maury had advanced some of the ideas of the series in his piece "Southern and Western Commerce." He described the "boundless commercial possibilities" of the Amazon River valley, whose basin "is but a continuation of the Mississippi Valley." He urged the free navigation of the Amazon, which at that moment was closed to all but Brazilian shipping. As he put it: "The right of our people to go with their Mississippi steamers into the Amazon will, when exercised, draw emigrants to that valley, who, being there, will become our best customers; and as soon as the proper impulse is given to their commerce and the industrial pursuits, we shall then find there, at our doors, instead of away on the other side of the world, all the productions of the East."[88]

Maury perceived the Amazon valley as a new New World ripe for development, a country "for the most part a wilderness of howling monkeys and noisy parrots." While its boundaries are fringed with settlements, as soon as one leaves the outskirts of the valley and penetrates into the interior only the merest traces of "civilized man" are found. His introduction to the first article asserted that the area, "if reclaimed from the savage, the wild beast, and the reptile, and reduced to civilization now, would be capable of supporting with its produce the population of the whole world."[89] Thus Maury's subtext was clearly the magisterial gaze of

Manifest Destiny now overspreading the continental borders.

Maury likened the Amazon waterway to the Mississippi as a potential source of commerce and wealth for the United States, evoking a magical paradise of luxuriant fertility and unlimited exportable commodities. Maury situated himself smack in the center of contemporary expansionist thought with his observation that the millions of square miles of the Amazon valley were more accessible to the United States than to most of South America itself and that the area could serve as a "safety valve" for the bourgeoning population of the Union (including "surplus" black workers from the Southern states who would provide the labor). Maury expressed anger over the Brazilian court's interdiction of American free use of the Amazon and gave vent to the militant Anglo-Saxonism that justified the Brazilian emperor's fears of the Yankee adventurers: "This miserable policy by which Brazil has kept shut up, and is continuing to keep shut up, from man's—from Christian, civilized, enlightened man's use of the fairest portion of God's earth, would be considered by the American people as a nuisance, not to say an outrage."[90] Then, in the standard cadences of the day, Maury sang the song of the magisterial gaze in its sweep across the Amazon valley:

> From the statements which I have already made, all must admit that the valley of the Amazon is not only a great country, but it is a glorious wilderness and waste, which, under the improvement and progress of the age, would soon be made to "blossom as the rose." We have, therefore, but to let loose upon it the engines of commerce—the steamer, the emigrant, the printing press, the axe, and the plough—and it will teem with life.[91]

Those words were calculated to enkindle the imagination of a visionary merchant, and Field resolved to visit and evaluate this vast new market for himself. But Field needed fellow travelers to confirm his discoveries and share in their communication. He chose Church as the person who could most vividly interpret their findings and arouse support for future plans through his visualizations of the South American landscape. While Field would collect the hard data and appraise the economic potential, Church would promote the scheme by projecting vast possibilities for thousands of spectators from the prospect of the magisterial gaze. Church had himself been stimulated by Maury's South American dithyrambs, and analogous to Field, he felt he had exhausted the possibilities of North America and now wanted to move on to greener pastures. What began as the expression of a sense of mastery in the Hudson River Valley now overspread the continent in an unlimited space allotted by Providence. Thus the landscapist Church did not simply go along for the ride but joined forces with the entrepreneur for the express purpose of translating Manifest Destiny into concrete terms.

Field's itinerary included visits to gold, silver, and emerald mines, waterfalls, and bridges, and it is no coincidence that Church's sketches from the trip embrace many otherwise mundane objects such as native products of tin and silver, mining tools, methods of harnessing water, details of bridge construction, manufactories, marketplaces, and methods of local transportation.[92] While Field collected actual samples of ore and artifacts, Church sketched them. An Aspinwall, New Granada (now Colón, Panama), paper of October 1853 had the two adventurers at their journey's end declaring in gushing language reminiscent of Maury that the scenery of the Andes was "grand and beautiful beyond description; . . . that gold in large quantities can be obtained in Antioquia, and from the beds of many of the small streams that run down the Andes into the Pacific or the

Amazon; and that the soil on the plains of Bogota and in the valley of the Cauca is very rich; and that they have been so pleased with their journey that they intend soon to return to the land of beautiful flowers and birds, and to the continent for which the Almighty has done so much and man so little."[93]

In this report their views are conjoined, and their common position demonstrates interlocking impressions of the landscape and the commercial potential of the land. Both Field and Church grasp the landscape in similar terms, suggesting their shared vision of the magisterial gaze. Church's serial depiction of smoldering Cotopaxi, the spectacular volcano of the Andes, metaphorically suggested a new world in the making, as well as one ripe for the plucking. Church first sketched it in the company of Field, and it was for the entrepreneur that he painted the breathtaking 1855 view of the volcano. It was in the very heart of the

Andes—as the itinerary demonstrates—that Field's dual fascination with geology and mining came together, and Church's imaginative projections could satisfy the patron's vision of the merger of science and industry. No one could doubt at the time that together they meant to arouse North American consciousness of the neglected potential of the South American continent and urge its exploitation as part of a vast scheme. Church's *Heart of the Andes*—the masterpiece of the expedition—responds to Maury's description of "the heart of the country" as "a commercial blank" attainable only "through the powers of steam and the free use of its majestic water-courses."[94]

Field's basically imperialist outlook is shown in his bringing back to his home an Indian youth of fourteen with the intention of educating him and sending him back to his native land as a missionary.[95] To Field, not only was the youth a specimen of the Amazon valley, akin to an animal, mineral, or agricultural product, but he also clearly figured in Field's plans as a case study for the domestication of the native culture and its ultimate exploitation in the name of the imperialist clichés of religion and civilization. Church, typically sympathetic to his patron's schemes, endorsed the bizarre idea, noting that "the boy is as efficient as most people here."[96]

Field's next project—the laying of the transatlantic cable—catapulted him from the rank of the merely successful to the pantheon of legendary daring adventurers.[97] Yet the cable scheme was a physical extension of his dream of Manifest Destiny, which he shared with the others in the group that helped finance and organize it. They included Marshall O. Roberts, the iron magnate Peter Cooper, Samuel Morse (artist and inventor of the telegraph), and Moses Taylor, a New York importer and later president of the City Bank, all self-made magnates whose self-esteem was rooted in their per-

sonal sense of unlimited opportunity and their historical vision of an unlimited field of action. As Cooper recalled the meeting in which Field outlined his plan, he immediately agreed to participate in the belief "that it offered the possibility of a mighty power for the good of the world."[98] Field himself arrived at the idea after listening to a Canadian plan to span the rugged territory of Newfoundland with a telegraph system; he then retired to his study and, contemplating the globe, spun the even more audacious scheme to lay a cable across the North Atlantic. An important photograph of the period shows him leaning on the globe in his study, signifying mastery of the planet (Fig. 17).

The attempt to achieve communication between two continents followed the return from South America. The connection between the two events is not one solely of chronology but of ideology as well. Field consulted Lieutenant Maury, the author of the articles on the

Amazon valley and chief of the Naval Observatory in Washington, D.C., concerning the geological and engineering problems of laying the cable across the ocean floor.[99] Maury's pioneering oceanographic studies supplied valuable information on the currents and soundings of the Atlantic. As in the case of the South American venture, Field insisted on the commercial and "remunerative" aspects of the electrical continental bridge. As he stated in his public circular, "The genius of science and the spirit of commerce alike demand, that the obstacles of geographical position and distance alone shall no longer prevent the accomplishment of such a union."

The initial achievement of the transatlantic cable in 1858 was hailed by Walt Whitman as the most significant event of the epoch, winning for Field "imperishable fame as the foremost man of the nineteenth century." Whitman was then ardently disposed to Manifest Destiny, and his essay "The Moral Effect of the

Fig. 17. Mathew Brady, photograph of Cyrus W. Field, 1860.

Cable" emphasizes the Anglo-Saxon triumphal march now led by the Yankee contingent: "It is the union of the great Anglo-Saxon race, henceforth forever to be a unit, that makes the States throb with tumultuous emotion and thrills every breast with admiration and triumph." [100] Whitman's gushing enthusiasm demonstrates the intimate connection of American expansionist thought with the transatlantic cable.

The large-scale entrepreneurial schemes and real estate ventures of Field and his protégé Church shed further light on the links between their real-time ventures and their personal fantasies. Not fortuitously, both built mansions overlooking the Hudson River and materialized the imaginative world projected by the landscapists. Wishing to live in a style appropriate to his purchasing power, the Anglophilic Field bought a country estate near Irvington, New York, that he named Ardsley,

after the English birthplace of John Field, a sixteenth-century astronomer. (His nearest neighbor was Jay Gould, the notorious stock-market swindler.) [101] He built a massive Victorian house with a wide veranda looking out across the Hudson to the Palisades, and almost fifty acres of wooded parkland surrounding the house sloped down to the river. The Fields built one of the largest greenhouses in the country on the estate, where they grew exotic plants from the tropics as well as domestic varieties, and fresh-cut flowers were sent almost daily to their New York City residence in Gramercy Park. Field continued to expand his property until he owned half a mile of frontage between Dobbs Ferry and Irvington. He now grouped his family around him in separate villas on nearly two hundred acres and then enlarged the Hudson River community by purchasing an additional five hundred acres in the Neperan Valley, whose residents became his tenants. The editor of the Tarreytown *Argus,* the local newspaper, could note the number of spectacular vistas controlled by the location of Field's property, and he reported that the summit of Field's estate "is a wildly beautiful spot in the very heart of the woods, and is reached by good carriage roads in different directions. It is said that on a clear day four States can be seen from that outlook." [102] Field's commercial empire and his life-style symbolically converged on the sighting from the summit of his estate.

Similarly, Church's entrepreneurial schemes and real estate ventures provide a real-life counterpart to his pictorial urge to earth mastery. He built a bizarre mansion on the east bank of the Hudson River (probably to compete with his rival Albert Bierstadt, whose villa overlooked Irvington-on-Hudson) that he named Olana, establishing architectural vantage points from which the vast panorama of the Catskill Moun-

tains could be surveyed and sketched. [103] As he began to amass the 126 acres of his eventual estate, he wrote a friend, "I want to secure every rood of ground that I shall ever require to make my farm perfect." Just before breaking ground for the eclectically exotic residence, he could exclaim with unabashed pride of ownership, "About an hour this side of Albany is the Center of the World—I own it." During his late years, when he found it difficult to paint, he turned to exploitation of his grounds to organize views as he had in the New England wilderness and in the jungles of Ecuador. He could even compare this activity favorably with the practice of landscape painting: "I have made about one and three-quarters miles of road this season, opening entirely new and beautiful views—I can make more and better landscapes in this way than by tampering with canvas and paint in the studio." [104] He would then ride about the estate in his carriage, gaz-

74

Fig. 18. Asher B. Durand, *Progress*, 1853. The Warner Collection, Gulf States Paper Corporation, Tuscaloosa, Alabama. (See color plate.)

ing at the prospects he had engineered for his visual enjoyment. Hence Church provides a case study of the artist-entrepreneur for whom the magisterial gaze constituted a blueprint for changing the world.

Asher B. Durand, Thomas Cole's close colleague, had provided the paradigmatic formulation of the magisterial gaze in a work of 1853 entitled, appropriately enough, *Progress* (Fig. 18).[105] Much more literal-minded and schematic than either Cole or Church, Durand encoded his concept of progress in readily identifiable terms for the dominant elite and their cultural representatives. Starting from the inevitable left-foreground *repoussoir* of the blasted trees and rude wilderness site, the diagonal line of sight takes off to the valley below, where every type of busy mercantile activity imaginable is paraded before the viewer. In this case, Durand added to the foreground motif a group of Native Americans peering out of the

wilderness upon the cultivated scene below. As one reviewer sounded the characteristic ambiguity of American progress, "The wild Indian is seen taking a last look at the land of his fathers, and for the last time treading those mountain glades, so beautiful in their wild scenery, but soon to change and disappear before the white man's resistless march of improvement." Not surprisingly, another critic of the period described the work as "purely AMERICAN. It tells an American story out of American facts, portrayed with true American feeling, by a devoted and earnest student of Nature."[106]

The diagonal line of sight is synonymous with the magisterial gaze, taking us rapidly from an elevated geographical zone to another below and from one temporal zone to another, locating progress synchronically in time and space. Within this fantasy of domain and empire gained from looking out and down over broad expanses is the subtext of metaphorical forecast of the future. The future is given a spatial location in which vast territories are brought under visual and symbolic control. Halfway down the slope we see a road along which drovers take their wares, leading to the manufacturing centers near the river speckled with the smoke of chimneys and steamships. A train in the middle distance crosses a viaduct moving west in the direction of the river toward the setting sun. (It was in 1853 that Congress passed the Pacific Railroad Survey bill for determining within ten months the most "practicable and economical" trans-Mississippi railroad route to the Pacific.[107]) Thus "progress" implies the conquest of empire as well, anticipating the visualization of the future in the image of the frontiersman surveying the western horizon from the heights of a mountain pass. The generation of patrons who supported Durand's Hudson River productions, like the New York merchant Luman Reed, would pass on the mantle to their younger business part-

ners, like Marshall O. Roberts, who also collected the painter of the Rockies, Albert Bierstadt.

I am convinced that Thomas Crawford's design for the eastern portico of the United States Capitol, executed the same year as *Progress,* embodies the identical concept (Fig. 19). The program was given by the engineer Captain Montgomery C. Meigs, the officer in charge of the extension of the Capitol (and later responsible for Leutze's commission). He explained the subject as one that would transcend class: "In our history of the struggle between civilized man and the savage, between the cultivated and the wild nature are certainly to be found themes worthy of the artist and capable of appealing to the feelings of all classes."[108] Crawford represented this theme diachronically, moving outward from the center toward the wings of the pediment. The central figure personifying America stands on a rock, with the sun rising behind her. (In this sense, she may

Fig. 19. Thomas Crawford, pediment on the east portico of the U.S. Capitol, marble. Architect of the Capitol, Washington, D.C.

be considered to be facing the direction of progress, that is, from civilization's boundary toward the wilderness.) She stretches her left hand in the direction of a pioneer who clears the forest and for whom she asks God's protection. A retreating rattlesnake signals the end of the wilderness, while the extinction of the Native Americans that is its corollary is depicted in the astonishment and despair of the Indian chief and his son. Crawford declared that in the image of the slumped chief, "I have endeavored to concentrate all the despair and profound grief resulting from the conviction of the white man's triumph."[109] And he even included an emblematic grave to complete the metaphor on that side of the tympanum. The opposite wing of the pediment is devoted to the advance of civilization in the wake of the pioneer, starting with the soldier in revolutionary costume (originally modeled after George Washington), who attests that "our freedom was obtained by the sword and must be preserved by it." Next comes the merchant whose right hand rests on the globe, "to indicate the extent of our trade," and he is followed by personifications of education, labor, and mechanized industry. The pediment on this end is terminated by sheaves of wheat, expressive of fertility, activity, and abundance to contrast with the emblem of Indian extinction at the opposite angle of the tympanum.

Here is the sculptural analogue to the painted landscape depictions of the magisterial gaze. The personification of a westward-facing America elevated on the rock in the center of the pediment occupies the position of the observer—"the all-seeing eye" of the pyramid—on the hill on which the lines of the visual cone converge. America, together with the symbolic Father of the Country alongside her, inhabits the lofty plane of Spirit. The magisterial trajectory radiates from a heady ambition that has introjected God as its ultimate source of inspiration. The sloping sides of the pediment are analogous to the trajectory tracing the widening of this divine view and the path of progress. Gradually, the wilderness gives way to culture and material domination and the displacement of the non-Christian indigenous people, who look upon the scene before them with wonderment and awe.

One of the favorite visual tropes of the period is that image of the stupefied savage confronting the signs of civilization on the march. It appears on bank notes as well as in the high art manifestations of painters like DeWitt Clinton Boutelle (1820–1884).[110] These popular images ranged from the hilltop occupants collapsing in total despair to the still proud warrior surveying the Anglo-Saxon encroachments with scorn (Figs. 20–23). Boutelle, born in Troy at the height of his namesake's popularity as father of the Erie Canal, lived out the myth underlying its construction. He painted up and down the Hudson, in the Catskills, in New Jersey, and on the Susquehanna, tracking the advance of commerce by way of contrast with

the last remnants of the vanishing natives. He set his Native American hunters on rocky ledges overlooking the Hudson River with its bustling activity of merchant ships and ferries and surrounded by farms and villages. Significantly, Boutelle's landscapes replicate the typical Hudson River arrangement but substitute a cigar-store Indian for the imagined spectator. Akin to Durand's *Progress* (which Boutelle's work antedates), the presence of this figure signifies the contest between wilderness and natives on the one hand and civilization and technology on the other. Whereas the earlier painters such as Cole merely suggested that contest in a blasted tree trunk or overgrown promontory, their heirs carefully spell out the message. Although the figure of the barbarian in this key position would seem to contradict my previous assertion about the view from the Godhead, in fact he is identified totally with the wilderness that is all but conquered. As in Crawford's scheme, he metaphorically points

Fig. 20. DeWitt Clinton Boutelle, *The Indian Hunter*,
1843. The Chrysler Museum,
Norfolk, Virginia. (See color
plate.)

Fig. 21. DeWitt Clinton Boutelle, *Indian Surveying a Landscape*, 1855. Gift of Martha C. Karolik for the M. and M. Karolik Collection of American Paintings, 1815–1865. Courtesy, Museum of Fine Arts, Boston.

Fig. 22. Anonymous, bank-note engraving, Rawdon, Wright, Hatch and Edson, New York, 1850s.

to one stage in the process of the advancing
frontier, as an incidental object in the line of
sight. Reviewing two landscapes by Jasper
Cropsey in 1847, the critic for the *Literary
World* clarified the role of the artist in record-
ing this evolution: "The axe of civilization is
busy with our old forests, and artisan ingenuity
is fast sweeping away the relics of our national infancy. . . . What were once the wild
and picturesque haunts of the Red Man, and
where the wild deer roamed in freedom, are becoming the abodes of commerce and the seats
of manufactures."[111]

In his "Letters on Landscape Painting,"
Durand admonished the neophyte not to
"seek the pursuit of Art for the sake of gain"
and thereby degrade art to the level of a
trade.[112] But his own practice contradicted his
preachments, including his early illustration
and bank-note work and his association with

Fig. 23. Anonymous, bank-
note engraving, Rawdon,
Wright, Hatch and Edson,
New York, 1850s.

wealthy merchants and railroad entrepreneurs whose business schemes he helped promote by word and deed. His other admonition to the young student, not to go abroad "in search of material for the exercise of your pencil, while the virgin charms of our native land have claims on your deepest affections," springs from his identification with the reigning elite, mainly former Jacksonian Democrats:

> I desire not to limit the universality of the Art, or require that the artist shall sacrifice aught to patriotism; but, untrammeled as he is, and free from academic or other restraints by virtue of his position, why should not the American landscape painter, in accordance with the principle of self-government, boldly originate a high and independent style, based on his native resources?[113]

Those "native resources" are there, of course, at the behest of the patron, who owns the land along the Hudson and in the wilderness regions. The "wild districts" may have yet been spared "the pollutions of civilization," but they make sense only in tandem with those pollutions that Durand so lovingly painted the year before the "Letters" were published in *Crayon*.

The magisterial gaze enabled the landscape painter to express this ardent nationalism through the distance it interposed between the pollutions and the land's former wild state. The magisterial gaze resolved the paradox of "the machine in the garden," linking the pastoral ideal with the wild and civilized zones as part of a visual and, therefore, historical transition. The need to retain the pastoral fantasy to counter the capitalist hegemony lies behind the drive to find new frontiers: each realization of civil and technical society betrays the fantasy, and hence the pressure to discover new ones—including the latest in outer space—to begin the lie all over again. The dream of a retreat to an unspoiled oasis of harmony and innocence

Thomas Cole, *Oxbow*
(*The Connecticut River near
Northampton*), 1836.

Frederic Edwin Church,
Mount Ktaadn, 1853.

Asher B. Durand, *Progress,* 1853.

DeWitt Clinton Boutelle,
The Indian Hunter, 1843.

Asher B. Durand,
Kindred Spirits, 1849.

Albert Bierstadt, *Domes of the Yosemite*, 1867.

John Mix Stanley, *Scouts in the Tetons*, 1860.

Emanuel Leutze, *Westward the Course of Empire Takes Its Way,* 1861. Mural study for United States Capitol. National Museum of American Art, Washington, D.C. Bequest of Sara Carr Upton.

has to be accompanied by the forces of civilization that alone can provide the means to attain it. Thus within the magisterial gaze the middle landscape is less a transcending idea than one of appendage—the park and the garden behind the manor house.

The key to this understanding is Durand's *Kindred Spirits,* one of the most popular works of the Hudson River school (Fig. 24).[114] It is a memorial to Thomas Cole executed the year after the master's death. It depicts Cole and the poet William Cullen Bryant—who delivered the eulogy at Cole's funeral—on a ledge overlooking a dramatic gorge in the Catskills. Although the composition is oriented vertically rather than horizontally and the two protagonists stand almost at right angles to the scene before them, Cole points with his brush in a direction that leads the eye through the landscape, akin to the previous examples. Durand has, in effect, constructed an allegory

of the magisterial gaze and made it the central theme of his painting. Although no conspicuous signs of industry or artifice mar the scenic beauty of the site, the names of Cole and Bryant are inscribed on a tree in the left foreground—suggesting glorified graffiti in the wilderness that now stamps it as their turf. We know what Cole and Bryant were thinking, because in their personal lives they chose sites to live in that suggested the idea of the wilderness in their back yards (Fig. 25). The cantilevered ledge on which they stand is no longer a platform of wilderness but in effect a surrogate terrace or balcony, providing a view from their dreamhouse. Indeed, the landscape is made noble by the very presence of the great men who above all others are able to assess its beauty. The work was commissioned by Jonathan Sturges, the younger partner of Luman Reed and Durand's faithful benefactor, and he presented it to Bryant as a gift.

86

Fig. 24. Asher B. Durand,
Kindred Spirits, 1849. Collec-
tion of The New York Public
Library, Astor, Lenox and Til-
den Foundations, New York.
(See color plate.)

Fig. 25. Granville Perkins,
*Mr. Bryant's Favorite Seat—
View from the Hall Door at Ros-
lyn,* 1878.

Three years after Durand painted that picture, George P. Putnam published *The Home Book of the Picturesque,* a collaborative enterprise by leading authors of New York and Hudson River artists in the service of the reigning elite.[115] It represents the cultural expression of the chauvinism in the wake of the Mexican War and the intoxicating sense of conquest and annexation. Putnam dedicates the book to Durand, then president of the National Academy and one of the illustrators of the book, with the message that the work is "an initiatory suggestion for popularizing some of the characteristics of American Landscape and American Art." The publisher announces at the outset,

> That American artists have ample scope for the development of genius, in the department of landscape painting, is a truism too self-evident to need any argumentative dissertations. A very laudable degree of success in the cultivation of this genius, is also evident in many of our private drawing-rooms, as well as public exhibitions.

Having established his audience, Putnam then goes on to explain the rationale of the publication:

> Believing that ample material thus exists for illustrating the picturesque beauties of American landscape, the publisher has ventured to undertake this volume as an experiment, to ascertain how far the taste of our people may warrant the production of home-manufactured presentation books, and how far we can successfully compete with those from abroad. In the higher range of ornamental books of this class, such as are sought for by our liberal, gift-giving people, we have heretofore depended almost exclusively upon our importations from Europe.[116]

Here we see quite clearly and candidly the folding of the landscape aesthetic into the cultural aspirations of the privileged class. As the undeveloped land is subjugated to development and speculation, landscape assumes a pregnant role in masking the commercialized objectives of those who promote it. The publisher in turn produces for a highly sophisticated market preoccupied with gaining economically on European markets, and thus rivals competition in his own field from abroad. The domination of the land and landscape through the magisterial gaze of Cole and Bryant conjures up the ineffable sense of domain through the metaphorical idea of being the master of all they survey. This occurs only in a purely American context that no longer has to depend on European imports for its economic and cultural life. Both the artists and their patrons equated indigenous material success with the prodigality of their home-grown landscape, and this nationalist equation was deliberately flaunted over and against European culture.[117] A decade after Putnam published his book critics could note that the

French painter Horace Vernet had declined Meigs's invitation to paint on the wall where Leutze depicted *Westward the Course of Empire:* "We now have an American picture, painted by an American artist, and it is one of which any American can be proud."[118]

The essays that follow Putnam's introduction and the accompanying illustrations (contributed by Durand and other Hudson River painters, including young Church) are part of the package. Most informative perhaps, because it is seemingly the most ethereal, is the essay entitled "Scenery and Mind" by the Reverend E. L. Magoon, close friend of Durand, Bryant, and the circle of patrons that supported them.[119] Magoon starts out by lauding Putnam's book as a production "of the highest order. The diversified landscapes of our country exert no slight influence in creating our character as individuals, and in confirming our destiny as a nation." He then establishes his thesis that landscape itself exists as a product of the elevated mind, and that this mind

is a focal point in the universe, a profoundly deep centre around which everything beautiful and sublime is arranged, and towards which, through the exercise of admiration, every refining influence is drawn. Wonderful, indeed, is the radiant thread that runs through every realm of outward creation, and enlinks all their diversified influences with the innermost fibres of the soul. This is the vital nerve by virtue of which the individual is related to the universe, and the universe is equally related to the individual. Through this, all physical powers combine to relieve spiritual wants. Earth contributes her fulness of wealth and majesty; air ministers in all the Protean aspects of beauty and sublimity; fire, permeating every thing graceful and fair, gleams before the scrutinizing eye with a light more vivid than the lightning blaze.[120]

This contribution ultimately has a divine origin and addresses all of creation: "The book of nature, which is the art of God, as Revelation is the word of his divinity, unfolds its innumerable leaves, all illuminated with glorious imagery, to the vision of his creature, man, and is designed to elevate or soothe him by such influences as emanate from foaming cataracts, glassy lakes, and floating mists." Thus nature, as divine revelation, exists only in relation to the mind beholding it.

But this book of revelation appears different to different minds and is not everywhere the same: to "gross minds" it is not "a quiet and awful temple, but . . . a plenteous kitchen, or voluptuous banqueting-hall." Thus this book is only truly understood when it reveals itself to the "votary in the most refined and suggestive form." Magoon's example is the Apollo Belvedere, a work "indescribably more natural than any rustic of Teniers, or any allegorical figure of Rubens." The ability to discern high art, however, depends on an "interpreter" to unmask the mysteries:

> The master-scenes of nature, however, like the masterpieces of transcendent art, require for the inexperienced, yet earnest admirer, an interpreter; to the lukewarm and careless they are ever partially, if not completely, incomprehensible. Like certain delicate plants, their essential beauties shrink under rough handling, and become dimness to the profanity of a casual glance; they unveil themselves most fully to the enraptured, and pour the effulgence of their splendid mysteries into the fixed eye of him only who gazes on the charms he has studiously sought, and adores for their own sake.[121]

Magoon's privileged spectator, refined and wealthy enough to hire an interpreter, occupies a special niche in the scheme of things: "In viewing magnificent scenes, the soul, expanded and sublimed, is imbued with a spirit of divinity, and appears, as it were, associated with the Deity himself." Indeed, the spectator Magoon has in mind sees nature from the perspective of Omnipotent Being:

> All eminent geniuses are close observers of rural objects, and enthusiastic admirers of imposing scenery. There can be no approximation towards universal development, save as one lays the entire universe under contribution to his personal cultivation. He must absorb into his expanded soul resources from every kingdom competent to render him a sovereign indeed over the realms of emotion and thought. He that would fortify a giant arm to sever an isthmus or tunnel mountains, as a pathway for the nations, or wield a giant mind that can quicken and mould the sentiments of other

men gigantic like himself, must habitually feed on that aliment which is won in stray gifts by whosoever will find, and which, when attained, constitutes "a perpetual feat of nectar'd sweets where no crude surfeit reigns."[122]

Here is the aesthetic rationale for the entrepreneurial-minded system builder as well as artist, the type of familiar nineteenth-century text that has its visual analogue in the magisterial gaze. Magoon adds that "all great passions are fed, and all great systems are projected in solitude." This disposition to look to the effusions of nature as the paradigm for novelty, grandeur, and innovation is "instinctive to superior minds." Hence the view from the top is also the male earthmover substituting for God.

That Magoon has his elite constituency in mind is demonstrated in his recollection of a statement of Pliny the Younger to the effect that he was never happier "than when he was indulging himself at his country seats, where in healthful leisure he wrote his works, and celebrated the views which his villas afforded." To Magoon almost

all the heroism, moral excellence, and ennobling literature of the world, has been produced by those who, in infancy and youth, were fostered by the influence of exalted regions, where rocks and wilderness are piled in bold and inimitable shapes of savage grandeur, tinged with the hues of untold centuries, and over which awe-inspiring storms often sweep with thunders in their train. This is the influence which more than half created the Shakspeares, Miltons, Wordsworths, Scotts, Coleridges, Irvings, Coopers, Bryants and Websters of the world.[123]

Next to mountains in their exalting impact is the related influence of oceans on the "national mind."

The infinite is most palpably impressed upon the boundless deep; and wherever thought is accustomed with unimpeded wing to soar from plains, or traverse opening vistas through towering hills, that it may hover over the azure waste of waters becalmed, or outspeed foamcrested billows in wildest storms, there will literature present the brightest lineaments and possess the richest worth.[124]

Magoon idolizes the Greeks, "lords of land and sea," hardy mountaineers who were inspired, but not imprisoned, by their mountains. Whenever a Greek "scaled a height, old Ocean, gleaming with eternal youth, wooed him to her embrace, in order to bear him to some happy island of her far-off domain."

Magoon emphasizes that a country's literature and art, as in the case of ancient Greece, are truly national to the extent that they reflect the national character, and here the natural scenery and climate are crucial since it is the features of the natural landscape that "give form and color to the thoughts and words of all creative minds." Magoon then connects the Anglo-American textual tradition with indigenous landscape and its ultimate superiority:

> Through the living speech, and over the speaking page of the Anglo-Saxon, and Anglo-American race, one can easily recognize the daily vicissitudes and fluctuating seasons,—those tines and hues of vernal beauty, summer promise, autumnal wealth, and wintry desolation,—those dimly shrouding mists which alternate with brilliant light,—and which render objects more lovely and harmonious to those who realize the invisible and perceive the spiritual, who unite all worlds in the comprehensive grasp of their imagination, and thus substantiate in effective use that which to others is only shadowy and remote.[125]

This capacity to "unite all worlds in the comprehensive grasp of their imagination" is unavoidably linked to the magisterial gaze:

> The human soul, thirsting after immensity, immutability, and unbounded duration, needs some tangible object from which to take its flight,—some point whence to soar from the present into the future, from the limited to the infinite,—and is likely to be most vigorous in its capacity and productions where such facilities abound.[126]

He then returns to the "soaring heights" of mountains, though "among the most palpable facts of earth, it is on them that we always seem to be most in the domain of fancy." Magoon asserts that it is "impossible to overstate our indebtedness" to mountainous formations, which, upheaved from the earth, substituted "for dead level plains." When we contemplate in the plains, "the globe appears youthful and imbecile; among crags and mountains, it exhibits energy and gravity of age. All primitive aspects indicate a deep solemnity, and generate invincible power. We feel the spirit of the universe upon us." In these regions, the superior mind acts as a prism through which "inanimate kingdoms and artificial lessons are converted into golden visions of thought and feeling." Magoon concludes his essay with the association of biblical narrative and high places, recalling that it was on them "that the only true God manifested himself to the Hebrews of old, and it was on them that the tremendous mysteries of redemption were accomplished."[127]

After the Reverend Mr. Magoon's wide-ranging and speculative discourse on the native scenery and its critical import to native interests, James Fenimore Cooper got down to business and specifically compared American and European scenery. His working definition has been often quoted, but it is worthwhile to recall it here: "The great distinction between

American and European scenery, as a whole, is to be found in the greater want of finish in the former than in the latter, and to the greater superfluity of works of art in the old world than in the new." [128] Using the aesthetic idea of the sketch and finish, Cooper picked up the theme of futurity—that the American wilderness is in a state of becoming rather than fixed and polished like a masterwork. In this he also accepted the wilderness as a temporary condition destined for improvement by the hands of the people. He did feel that the mountains around Lake Como were incomparable and that nothing like them existed in North America. He made exception of the Rocky Mountains but noted the lack of human artifice to give the region its finishing touches: "The Rocky Mountains, and the other great ranges in the recent accession of territory, must possess many noble views, especially as one proceeds south; but the accessories are necessarily wanting, for a union

of art and nature can alone render scenery perfect." [129] He made no exception here: even in the case of Niagara Falls, the spectacular site "is scarcely more imposing than she is now rendered lovely by the works of man." He even exulted in the ability to penetrate "its very mists by means of a small steamboat." Hence for Cooper the wilderness gaze from the summit promises only good things to come in the way of transformation of the wild into the civilized. Cooper, who repeatedly leads his reader up a mountain overlooking the scene to be described, even uses the device to discuss French landscape: "It often occurs in that country that the traveller finds himself on a height that commands a view of a great extent, which is literally covered with *bourgs* or small towns and villages. In such places it is no unusual thing for the eye to embrace, as it might be in a single view, some forty or fifty cold, grave looking, chiselled *bourgs* and villages, almost invariably erected in stone."[130] The difference between that sight and a typical one in the United States is "the greater natural freedom that exists in an ordinary American landscape, and the abundance of detached fragments of wood, often render the views of this country strikingly beautiful when they are of sufficient extent to conceal the want of finish in the details which require time and long-continued labor to accomplish." One of his cherished dreams involved mountain views overlooking the progress of civilization in America: "We are of opinion that as civilization advances, and the husbandman has brought his lands to the highest state of cultivation, there will be a line of mountain scenery extending from Maine to Georgia, in a north and south direction, and possessing a general width if from one to two hundred miles, from east to west, that will scarcely have a parallel in any other quarter of the world."[131] Returning to his main thesis, he concluded that compared with "old, mature

Europe," America can claim "the freshness of a most promising youth," like a first sketch.

Cooper's daughter also contributed an essay, one that agrees in most essentials with her father's and draws on his novels for its imaginative background.[132] Still, it presents in her own voice the concept I call the magisterial gaze. Though the gaze is predominantly that of a property-owning male, it is not necessarily gender-based. Historically, however, the female spectator on the summit takes in the sites (sights) of the patriarchal culture. Recalling a hazy October morning on a projecting cliff, "which overlooked the country for some fifteen miles or more; the lake, the rural town, and the farms in the valley beyond, lying at our feet like a beautiful map," Susan Cooper thinks of the wilderness in terms of seasonal experience, preferring it in winter or summer but never in autumn. In October "let us return to a peopled region." As if seeing before her a Hudson River painting, she continues,

A broad extent of forest is no doubt necessary to the magnificent spectacle, but there should also be broken woods, scattered groves, and isolated trees; and it strikes me that the quiet fields of man, and his cheerful dwellings, should also have a place in the gay picture. Yes; we felt convinced that an autumn view of the valley at our feet must be finer in its present varied aspect, than in past ages when wholly covered with wood.

And she goes on to conclude,

The hand of man generally improves a landscape. The earth has been given to him, and his presence in Eden is natural; he gives life and spirit to the garden. It is only when he endeavors to rise above his true part of laborer and husbandman, when he assumes the character of creator and piles you up hills, pumps you up a river, scatters stones, or sprinkles cascades, that he is apt to fail. Generally the grassy meadow in the valley, the winding road climbing the hillside, the cheerful village on the bank of the stream, give a higher additional interest to the view; or where there is something amiss in the scene, it is when there is some evident want of judgment, or good sense, or perhaps some proof of selfish avarice, or wastefulness, as when a country is stripped of its wood to fill the pockets or feed the fires of one generation. [133]

Henry T. Tuckerman's essay, "Over the Mountains, or the Western Pioneer," unequivocally connects the "immensity of the prospect" of the Alleghenies with national futurity. [134] The intrepid pioneer annexed the landscape, boldly going "'over the mountains', to clear a pathway, build a lodge, and found a state in the wilderness." Tuckerman then recalls a picture by William Ranney in the American Art-Union gallery in New York that articulated this connection, "so thoroughly national in its subject."

It represented a flat ledge of rock, the summit of a high cliff that projected over a rich, umbrageous country, upon which a band of hunters leaning on their rifles, were gazing with looks of delighted surprise. The foremost, a compact and agile, though not a very commanding figure, is pointing out the landscape to his comrades, with an air of exultant yet calm satisfaction; the wind lifts his thick hair from a brow full of energy and perception; his loose hunting shirt, his easy attitude, the fresh brown tint of his cheek . . . proclaim the hunter and pioneer, the Columbus of the woods, the forest philosopher and brave champion. The picture represents Daniel Boone discovering to his companions the fertile levels of Kentucky.[135]

Tuckerman then notes that Boone, by profession a surveyor and Indian fighter, laid out the infant settlement of what later would become the state capital.

One essayist for the *Home Book* merits special recognition, if only to bring to light a once popular travel writer now relegated to the dustbin of history: Bayard Taylor.[136] A protégé of Nathaniel Willis (who wrote a laudatory preface to the young author's first book, *Views Afoot*), Taylor was an indefatigable writer, lecturer, traveler, and public relations expert for expansionism. As an amateur painter who once considered becoming a landscapist (he even exhibited work at the National Academy), he associated himself with every important landscape artist and writer in the orbit of his publisher George Putnam. Putnam had profited enormously from the sale of Taylor's travel writings [137] and commissioned his pieces "The Scenery of Pennsylvania" (Taylor's native state) and "The Erie Railroad" [138] to enhance the commercial appeal of the *Home Book*. Taylor was no sentimentalist when it came to the railways, and he decried the "vulgar lament" over the so-called "merciless embodiments of the Present and the Practical." Indeed,

We shall learn, ere long, that no great gift of science ever diminishes our stores of purer and more spiritual enjoyment, but rather adds to their abundance and gives them a richer zest. Let the changes that *must* come, come: and be sure they will be bringing us more than they take away.[139]

Taylor sees the route of the Erie Railroad possessing all the advantages of creature comforts without sacrificing any of the sites "where the poetry of the Past still lives." Nevertheless, it represents the wave of the future: it is the longest road in the world, and on a small scale represents "the crossing of a continent." It belts four dividing ridges of mountains, separating five different systems of rivers and streams, and yet requires no inclined plane or tunnel. What distinguishes it above all other railroads is its "apparent disregard of natural difficulties."[140] In short, the railroad, and especially the Erie line, is the material realization of the magisterial gaze.

Taylor was the popular spokesman for the genteel elite who supported the new expression of the national landscape.[141] Although he was born in a small Quaker town in Pennsylvania, Taylor's life and career point to a need to escape that modest environment and its provincial values. He established his early national reputation on the basis of his European travel sketches for two New York newspapers, anthologized in his *Views Afoot,* a book that went through twenty editions in a decade. He parlayed his reputation as world traveler into a full-time career as writer and lecturer; on the lecture circuit he drew crowds even in small country towns. Taylor's strenuous exertions were aimed at accumulating enough capital to build a great manor house in the hills of his native Kennett Square.

Taylor's cosmopolitanism went only skin deep: he spoke for the dominant Anglo-Saxon elite of the Northeast. When in Africa he mistakenly assumed that the ancient Ethiopians had descended from the Caucasian race, and he found it gratifying "that the highest Civilization, in every age of the world, has been developed by the race to which we belong." [142] Even though he could severely criticize the imperialism of the East India Company, he managed to justify it as necessary to the advance of civilization. Like the Yankee imperialists as well, Taylor's preference was always for civilization against nature—except, of course, for the dense urban kind when it came too close for comfort; then Taylor felt the need to pack his bags once again and "escape from everything that could remind me of the toil and confusion of the bewildering world." [143]

Taylor was a world traveler not only in the generic but also in the specific sense. He seems to be everywhere at once in the nineteenth century, and what makes him such an appealing case study is his sphere of contacts among the robber barons, entrepreneurs, writers, and artists who make up my narrative. He knew intimately Bierstadt, Worthington Whittredge, Gifford, and Church and served as intermediary between Church and Alexander von Humboldt, whom he could also claim as a close friend. [144] Railroad entrepreneurs invited him to ride the maiden voyages of their lines and could always count on him for a positive review in the New York *Tribune*. A fellow member with Matthew Maury and Cyrus Field in the American Geographical Society, Taylor enthusiastically endorsed their plans for a transatlantic cable. He was invited to join and chronicle the Field expedition in 1854 to lay the submarine cable between Newfoundland and Cape Breton, the preliminary stage in spanning the North Atlantic. [145] Taylor's travel books and poetry—which earned him the title "The American Traveler"—expressed in literary guise the tension of the dominant elite between their desire to organize and discipline the vast unruly landscape and their need to escape from the very boundaries that they helped determine.

Taylor's Protestant ethic had been given cultural expression by the landscapists, rendering American scenery for an Anglo-Saxon elite in the idiom of glory and power. On his way to the White Mountains, Taylor noted that much of the landscape "consisted of remembrances of New York studios. Every foreground was made up of sketches by Shattuck, Coleman, and the younger painters: every background was a complete picture by Kensett." [146] When he finally attained the summit of the White Mountains, he confessed that the pleasure he felt derived not alone from the beauty of the unfurling panorama below but also from a

> lurking, flattering sense of power, which we feel, although it may not consciously float on the surface of our emotions. We are elevated above the earth: other men and their concerns are below us: their stateliest possessions are insignificant patches, which we look down upon without respect or envy. Our own petty struggles and ambitions fade away also in the far perspective. We stand on the pinnacle of the earth, whereof we are lords, and above us there is nothing but God. [147]

That Taylor's coded viewpoint could be communicated to his contemporaries and shared with them is seen in Thomas Hicks's portrait of the author in 1855, during his travels to the Middle East (Fig. 26). Hicks depicted Taylor in Ottoman costume with an outsized turban and holding the long, flexible stem of a hookah. Although Taylor sought out what were for Americans strange customs as an antidote to the "fiends of gold and work," he nevertheless retained the sense of Yankee superiority during his Middle East adventures. [148] Taylor assumes the position of a potentate waited on by a servant, seated on an elevated terrace overlooking a commanding view of Damascus and Lebanon in the remote distance. The choice of viewpoint and presentation of

Fig. 26. Thomas Hicks, *Bayard Taylor,* 1855. National Portrait Gallery, Smithsonian Institution, Washington, D.C.

Taylor as symbolic master can hardly be coincidental, and we may well conclude that he dictated the pose and composition.

Taylor's preoccupation with land ownership is a microcosmic case of the larger drive for national conquest. His revealing essay in another work, "How I Came to Buy a Farm," tells a good deal about the mentality of those who worked on the *Home Book*.[149] Taylor came into ownership of a tract of eighty acres in Chester County, Pennsylvania, in 1853, the same year *Progress* was painted by Durand, a good friend and fellow member of the exclusive Century Association.[150] Taylor had always dreamed of this land adjoining his father's property, and as he returned home after a lengthy voyage he eagerly sought to claim it:

> Presently I recognized the boundaries of *my property*—yes, I actually possessed a portion of the earth's surface! After all, I thought, possession—at least so far as Nature is concerned— means simply *protection*. This moonlit wilderness is not more beautiful to my eyes than it was before; but I have the right, secured by legal documents, to preserve its beauty. I need not implore the woodman to spare those trees: I'll spare them myself. This is the only difference in my relation to the property. So long as any portion of the landscape which pleases me is not disturbed, I possess it quite as much as this.[151]

As he approaches the boundary, he imagines a chorus of the trees welcoming him as "our master and our preserver!" Suddenly, a new sensation sweeps over him, akin to the exhausted swimmer just touching ground: "My life had now a *point d'appui,* and, standing upon these acres of real estate, it seemed an easier thing to move the world. A million in bank stock or railroad bonds could not have given me the same positive, tangible sense of property."[152]

As Taylor crosses the threshold of his

fields, he posits his new condition as the basis of a solidarity of like-minded proprietors:

> Yes, one cannot properly be considered as a member of the Brotherhood of Man, an inhabitant of the Earth, until he possesses a portion of her surface. . . . The Agrarians, Communists, Socialistic Levellers, and Flats of all kinds, are replenished from the ranks of the non-owners of real estate. Banks break; stocks and scrips of all kinds go up and down on the financial see-saw; but a fee-simple of solid earth is THERE! You see it, you feel it, you walk over it. It is yours and your children's and their progeny's (unless mortgaged and sold through foreclosure) until the Millennium.[153]

But once he comes into actual ownership, his initial idealism slowly evolves into the insatiability of a landlord who balks at the presence of boundaries. Whereas before the only change in his relation to the land had to do with his exclusive right to preserve it intact, now he sees that within the limits of the tract "the proprietor is sovereign lord" and free to "build, tear down, excavate, fill up, plant, destroy, or do whatever else he will."

At this point, the magisterial gaze enters into his thinking and takes over: he notes that the ridge running through his property "commands an extensive view over the regions to the east, south, and west," carrying his prospect way beyond his boundary line. His previous exalted state of ownership is now displaced by a sense of discontent and "unreasonable longing: 'If all that were only mine!'" Like the frustrated child who cries because he has only one apple instead of six, Taylor

> now wanted to feel myself the owner of all the land within the range of vision. My possession was incomplete—it was only *part of a landscape.* Those forests which now so beautifully feather the distant hills may be destroyed at the will of another. I have no power to preserve them. How fortunate are those large landholders in England, who can ride thirty miles in a

straight line through their own property! They can mount the highest hill, and all which the rounded sky incloses belongs to them—stream, forest, meadow, mountain, village, mills, and mines! [154]

Here Taylor indicates that he is less interested in preserving the land than in the power implied by ownership, although he comes to this realization only when it is time to build his house. Gradually, reality catches up with his heady ambition, and he realizes that even if he were to own all the land within his vision he could never satisfy his longings, because there would always be another horizon beyond. Finally, he makes an imaginative leap to compensate for his dissatisfaction, still retaining the need for control over vast territories beyond his boundaries:

> Besides, I thought, this is but the *outside* of my farm. Possession is not merely the superficial area: it extends, legally, to the centre of the earth. I own, therefore, a narrow strip of terri-

tory nearly four thousand miles in length! Truly, I cannot travel to the end of my dominion; what of that?—I have no desire to do so. And above me, the seas of blue air, the dark, superimposing space—all is mine, half-way to the nearest star, where I join atmospheres with some far-off neighbor! The scattered clouds, as they pass over, the rain, the rainbow, lightnings and meteoric fires, become my temporary chattels. Under my feet, what unknown riches may not exist!—beds of precious minerals, geodes of jewels, sparry caverns, sections of subterranean seas, and furnaces heated from the central fire! This is wealth which, indeed, would not be received as collateral security for a loan, but it is therefore none the less satisfactory to the imagination. [155]

No passage in all of nineteenth-century American literature can more vividly demonstrate the relationship between metaphor and desire, between the magisterial gaze and the poetics of landscape. When it comes time to think about his country seat, Taylor reverts to his real ambition. He decides to plant shrubbery to hide his line fence from sight, and then he comes to "possess the entire landscape. The flag of the undivided union floats from my tower, and no traitor's footsteps have blackened my door-sill."

Taylor's will to mastery over the land makes him a member of an exclusive brotherhood—the heirs of those who backed the policy of Indian removal that cleared the land for white occupancy between the Appalachians and the Mississippi, cleared it for expansion, emigration and immigration, canals, railroads, new cities, and the building of a huge continental empire stretching to the Pacific Ocean. He tells us that his "soil shall be free" for all but some exceptions: "Hypocritical, insincere, time-serving creatures, shams of all kinds, men with creaky boots, stealthy cat-step, oily faces, and large soft hands, (which they are always rubbing)—for such there is no entrance." [156] Thus he means to make his soil free not in the narrow political sense but in the larger sense: "If I am lord of my own acres . . . I can certainly establish my own social laws." His model guest would be "Mr. H., the young Virginian Christian." [157]

We know that his exclusive club would not have included Jews, African Americans, Chinese, and Italians. Of the first group he wrote, "There is something . . . about a Jew, whether English or German, which marks him from all others. . . . It lays principally in [his] high cheek-bones, prominent nose and thin, compressed lips, which, especially in elderly men, give a peculiar miserly expression that is unmistakable." [158] As for Chinese—one of three disadvantages of a California journey including jolts and dust—Taylor wrote,

> The proximity of a greasy, filthy Chinaman, with his yellow libidinous face and sickening smell of stale opium, is in itself sufficient to poison all the pleasure of the journey. I have

often felt an involuntary repulsion when seated near a negro in some public conveyance, at home; but I confess I would rather be wedged in between two of the blackest Africans than be touched by one Chinaman. In both cases, the instinct is natural and unconquerable; but on the score of humanity, the former race stands immeasurably above the latter.[159]

Taylor, of course, seems to have momentarily forgotten that it was the Chinese who were building the railroads that contributed to his living. Elsewhere Taylor wrote that he could "distinguish between a Chinaman, a Negro, an Indian, and a member of the Caucasian race, in a perfectly dark room, by the sense of smell alone. The human blossoms of our planet are not all pinks and roses; we find also the *datura stramonium,* the toad's flax, and the skunk-cabbage."[160] Here the racism of Manifest Destiny is made stridently manifest.

Taylor traveled more than once to the

West Coast in pursuit of the American dream, the first time during the Gold Rush in 1849. While in San Francisco he purchased a piece of real estate overlooking the San Francisco Bay, a tract of two acres. It lacked grass and water, but it possessed "a magnificent prospect. At that time, I could scarcely say that I owned anything; and the satisfaction which I felt in sitting upon one of *my* rocks, and contemplating the view from my imagined front-window, amply repaid me for the surveyor's fee."[161] Ten years later, during a lecture tour around San Jose, he dreamed of retiring to the area in the future when the trip from New York to San Jose would be but a five-day journey. The cars would be traveling hotels and speed on an "unbroken line of rail from the Mississippi to the Pacific." Then would he purchase a property on the lowest slope of the surrounding mountains, overlooking the uncultivated, forested valley, and with a distant gleam of the bay. Dreaming farther into the future, he foresaw that the wild magnificence of raw nature in the valley would be "humming with human life" from riverbed to mountain summit. He saw the same oaks and sycamores of the old woods,

> but their shadows fell on mansions which were as fair as temples, with their white fronts and long colonnades: I saw gardens, refreshed by gleaming fountains,—statues peeping from the gloom of laurel bowers—palaces, built to enshrine the new Art which will then have blossomed here—culture, plenty, peace, happiness everywhere. I saw a more beautiful race in possession of this paradise—a race in which the lost symmetry and grace of the Greek was partially restored—the rough, harsh features of the original type gone—milder manners, better-regulated impulses, and a keener appreciation of all the arts which enrich and embellish life.[162]

Taylor's dazzling vision of utopia coincides, ironically, with the tensest period in the history of the Union, soon to witness the exhaustion of energies unleashed by Manifest Destiny in the orgiastic violence of the Civil War. This final flowering of the magisterial gaze receives its most self-conscious projection in Jasper Cropsey's veritable tour de force, *Autumn—On the Hudson River* (Fig. 27).[163] It stretches the panoramic format and directional gaze to the breaking point, an attempt to outdo the stereotype by exaggerating all the basic components. The wilderness zone now reaches across the entire width of the picture, while the viewer is led down a seemingly interminable slope to the town of Newburgh by a winding stream that turns into the Hudson and thence across its wide expanse by the brilliant, cloud-screened sunlight, whose reflections in the water link heaven and earth. Cropsey's operatic projection of the magisterial gaze attempts to gain maximum distance from the conflicts and factionalism that tore at the heart of the Union on the eve of the Civil War. The

Fig. 27. Jasper Francis Crop-sey, *Autumn—On the Hudson River,* 1860. National Gallery of Art, Washington, D.C. Gift of the Avalon Foun-dation.

enormous topographic expanse seeks to establish the idea of a beneficent order of nature vast enough to absorb the contradictions of a competitive society.

Painted in 1859–60, its declamatory style is understandable when we learn that he designed this monumental showpiece for an English public. Cropsey and his wife traveled to London in 1856, and he immediately went to work painting American landscapes for the English art market. Following the successful precedent of Church, whose *Niagara* and *Heart of the Andes* were shown to enthusiastic crowds in London in the late 1850s, Cropsey exhibited his painting in his studio and later in a gallery in Pall Mall. He received the support of Ruskin, who overcame an initial hesitation at what he suspected to be exaggerated presentations of American topography to enthusiastically endorse the painter. The one-picture show was reviewed in English journals steadily from March

through July 1860. Cropsey's landscape spectacle gave the critics healthy clues to his intention, as in the case of the reviewer who claimed that "the scene, which possesses a grand wildness, mixed with indications of advancing civilization and industry, present[s] a combined effect impossible to surpass."[164]

Cropsey's circular for the exhibition in Pall Mall described the landscape's vantage point, the west bank of the Hudson River, between West Point and Newburgh—the by now stereotyped section of the Hudson discussed in every album of American scenery. The flier also signaled the residence of none other than Nathaniel Parker Willis in the middle ground. Thus Cropsey's formula for appeal to a British public was to declaim the quintessential Yankee motif in stentorian terms. He gauged his audience correctly, for on the basis of the work's success Cropsey was presented to Queen Victoria in 1861, and the following year the painting was selected for inclusion in the London International Exhibition. That November Cropsey sold the painting for the highest price he had received to date.

Jasper Cropsey's *The Valley of Wyoming,* done just after the end of the Civil War, methodically attempts to conceal the implications of historical conflict and yet construct an image of property relations that are enhanced by the nostalgic residue of that conflict (Fig. 28).[165] The work was commissioned in 1864 by Milton Courtright, a civil engineer who later became president of the New York Elevated Railroad Company. Courtright grew up in the Wyoming Valley region and wanted a painting of his childhood home and its surroundings. Cropsey's search for the best view took its cue from a local historian named Charles Miner, who wrote in 1845 that the region differed substantially from its appearance in 1778, when it had been "a perfect Indian paradise."

The date 1778 is no arbitrary piece of periodization but refers specifically to an event that occurred in the region, a battle of the American War for Independence in which an army of Native American and British troops rushed the local settlements in the name of Pennsylvania and Connecticut territorial rights. The resulting carnage of this fierce attack was known forever after as the Wyoming Massacre and etched itself deeply into the collective memory of the local inhabitants. Cropsey knew it, since he affixed a plaque to the picture's frame carrying lines from a Scottish poet, Thomas Campbell, whose poem entitled "Gertrude of Wyoming" (1809) includes a recounting of the event. The narrative of the poem is set in the Wyoming Valley, and its cast encompasses the British-born Gertrude, her widowed father, Albert, the Native American chief Outalassi, and his ward, Waldegrave, an American youth who loves Gertrude. Waldegrave

Fig. 28. Jasper Francis Cropsey, *The Valley of Wyoming*,
1865. The Metropolitan Museum of Art, New York City.
Gift of Mrs. John C. Newing-
ton, 1966.

and Gertrude are eventually married, but wise Outalassi warns them to flee an impending invasion of English troops. Waldegrave's loyalty to the region predisposes him to ignore the chief's warning, and in the end he witnesses the death of his bride and her father in the ensuing massacre.

This old-fashioned Enlightenment morality play of pastoral love condemned to a tragic conclusion in the mad scramble for empire is recast by Cropsey in a specifically American mode. The first six lines establish the leitmotiv of the painting:

> On Susquehanna's side, fair Wyoming!
> Although the wild-flower on thy ruin'd wall
> And roofless homes, a sad remembrance bring
> Of what thy gentle people did befall;
> Yet thou wert once the loveliest land of all
> That see the Atlantic wave their morn restore.

Cropsey's foreground depicts a rough clearing in the woods with lounging farmers and grazing cows, thus emphasizing the pastoral as against the typical wilderness zone invariably associated with Native Americans. The view from this high plateau traces a sweeping visual path encompassing the Susquehanna River, the improved farmlands in the valley, and the thriving town of Plains, whose smoking industries are cozily nestled within the patchwork quilt of agrarian development. Cropsey creates an image of rural peace and balance achieved through civilization and culture, thus restoring the harmony that had existed on the eve of the massacre. But if the implications of conflict with Native Americans are evaded, Cropsey invokes nostalgia for the primitive to infuse his work with the feeling of the sublime. The systematic destruction of the Native Americans in Pennsylvania may be justified by reducing them to the barbarians of the Wyoming Massacre episode and at the same time be exploited as a silent signifier of the good old days that can never be recovered. Yet the longing for those days as an escape from the restrictions of civilization marks this commission by a civil engineer who in fact couldn't go home again.

For what has also been elided from this idyllic image of the state of Pennsylvania, drained north and south by the Susquehanna, is the history of conflict between the North and South brought dramatically to the doorstep of the state one year before the picture was commissioned. The Confederate Army of Northern Virginia invaded Pennsylvania in an effort to gain control of the key routes from the South leading to the state's major towns. The legendary showdown at Gettysburg proved to be one of the bloodiest battles in American history, but what is less well known is that at least one third of the ninety thousand troops on the Union side were native-born Pennsylvanians. Hence Cropsey's expansive picture of unbroken harmony and unity signifies the further absorption of loss and sacrifice into the grand scheme of Union.

Manifest Destiny's association with the spread of slavery and wartime trauma undercut its contribution to magisterial gazing. Yet this way of seeing the landscape hardened into a visual and literary stereotype that persisted deep into the twentieth century. In a remarkable testament to the tenaciousness of this cultural image, the advertising firm of N. W. Ayer and Son ran an ad in the 6 March 1926 issue of the *Saturday Evening Post* entitled "The Widened Vision," showing a pioneer with axe and coonskin cap standing on a hill overlooking a fertile valley cut by a winding river (Fig. 29). The pioneer gazes into the future, represented by a visionary urban skyline crowned with a rainbow, as if to suggest that the central goal of

Fig. 29. Ad for N. W. Ayer and Son, *Saturday Evening Post,* 6 March 1926, p. 97. Courtesy N. W. Ayer, Inc.

Fig. 30. John Mix Stanley,
*Oregon City on the Willamette
River,* ca. 1848. Amon Carter
Museum, Fort Worth, Texas.

the frontierspeople had been a towering sky-scraper city. The ad speaks with the rhetoric of Taylor, paying tribute to the "far-seeing men" who envisioned "a mighty nation rising from tangled woods and fertile plains." [166]

As fanciful as this picture might seem, it had been anticipated in the numerous nineteenth-century works depicting the magisterial gaze, in which the once forested valleys below have been transformed into flourishing towns. John Mix Stanley, an artist who participated in Western survey expeditions at midcentury, painted the panorama of Oregon City seen from the heights that still includes the standard Indian group as a foil for the march of progress (Fig. 30). Later, such views would show even more fully developed cities, as in Paul Frenzeny and Jules Tavernier's *Denver from the Highlands,* in which the indigenous peoples have been replaced by fashionably dressed men and women

picnicking on the heights and riding carriages up a mountain road (Fig. 31), or Cropsey's *Narrows from Staten Island,* where this time an artist surrounded by a group of admirers occupies the hilltop (Fig. 32).

These pictures differ fundamentally from the older schematic renderings of metropolitan centers spread out along a horizontal plane as if seen from a lofty point. Eighteenth-century and earlier bird's-eye views show straight-on panoramas without focus and without an organizing diagonal. [167] They are more closely related to the theatrical panoramas that offered no single vantage point for the constantly advancing viewpoint. [168] By contrast, the later images invariably orient the viewer along a predominant trajectory that may be considered the landscape's line of sight.

It is this line of sight that may be read as ideological, as in the singular instance of

Fig. 31. Paul Frenzeny and Jules Tavernier, *Denver from the Highlands*, 1874. Denver Public Library, Western History Department.

Fig. 32. Jasper F. Cropsey, *The Narrows from Staten Island,* 1870. Amon Carter Museum, Fort Worth, Texas.

Fig. 33. Robert Duncanson,
*View of Cincinnati, Ohio, from
Covington, Kentucky,* 1858.
Courtesy of The Cincinnati
Historical Society, Cincinnati.

Robert Duncanson's *View of Cincinnati, Ohio, from Covington, Kentucky* of 1858 (Fig. 33). Although Duncanson retains the standard progression from primitive zone of thickets, underbrush, and blasted trunks through the clearing of the farmer to the prospering city on the distant horizon, he varies the formula considerably by identifying both the wilderness and urban zones with topographical specificity. At the far right, on the hill between the trees, is the Mitchel (Mount Adams) Observatory, and below it, right above the treeline, are the supports of the bridge crossing the Licking River between Covington and Newport, Kentucky. The clearing along the shore on the opposite side of the Ohio River, where the boats are moored, is the Cincinnati Public Landing. The sharp bend of the river past the west side of town also squares with the topographical data. Thus the view is no longer so abstract

and schematic, and by contrasting the more rudimentary areas of Covington with the advanced culture of Cincinnati, Duncanson clearly drew a moral about the relative civilization of the two towns.

Duncanson based his composition on a daguerreotype, an engraving of which was reproduced in *Graham's Magazine* of June 1848 (Fig. 34). Both Duncanson and the photographer were black, and it is no coincidence that the central figure of the composition is a black farmer who occupies the middle zone between wilderness and town. The farmer leans on his scythe while chatting with two white children, who listen with respect to what he tells them. Farther down the hill we see his log cabin and his wife nearby, who hangs out her laundry to dry. Either they are slaves making use of Sunday free time or, what is more likely, they are freed, inhabiting the

Fig. 34. Engraving of view of
Cincinnati after a daguerreotype, 1848.

periphery of the town of Covington. (At the time of this painting, Covington's population consisted of about fifteen thousand whites, one hundred slaves, and fifty free colored.) It is proverbial that Kentucky's slaves looked to Cincinnati as their refuge from oppression, and those fortunate few who escaped from their condition did so via Covington during the winter when the Ohio River froze over. Thus Duncanson's retooling of the old formula takes the magisterial gaze as an evolutionary movement along the line of progressive emancipation of African Americans. In that sense, the wilderness tract is a metaphor for the interior thralldom of the border state that gradually opens out to the enlightened city on the opposite shore. Thus the black farmer stands in for the old pioneer who gradually clears the wilderness of malignancy on the way to freedom and civilization.

THE METALLIC LINE OF LEAST RESISTANCE

It is no coincidence that the clandestine route for transporting slaves to free territory was called the underground railroad. The straightest line of least resistance over and through every natural obstacle was the railway, and it thus became the metaphor for emancipation. The railroad magnates, however, had their own agenda: they were interested in enhancing property values and developing land for speculation. Their object was less a direct profit from their investment in the railroad than the construction of a major thoroughfare that increased the value of the land around it and enlarged the market for industry. Their machine's success, however, was fueled by the public relations campaign that brought it into congruence with the prevailing sense of inevitable expansion.

Fig. 35. Jasper Francis Cropsey, *Starrucca Viaduct, Pennsylvania*, 1865. The Toledo Museum of Art, Toledo, Ohio. Gift of Florence Scott Libbey.

Hence the ease by which the chartered companies enlisted the talents of the painters and photographers to publicize their projects.[169]

The role of the Eastern landscapists was to tame the wild beast and put it out to pasture. For Leo Marx, "the machine in the garden" exemplified the "assimilability" of the new technology, occupying the middle ground between wilderness zone and town.[170] Actually, this should be seen in dynamic rather than static terms, as a transition stage on the way to the New Athens, the New Rome, or the New Jerusalem. The image of the railroad winding its way down from the summit represented the actualization of the abstract gaze into its concrete and iron manifestation. Jasper Cropsey's *Starrucca Viaduct* depicts a view of the most famous bridge on the route of the New York and Erie Railroad, once known as the Eighth Wonder of the World (Fig. 35). An immense structure of hewn stone, 1,200 feet long and 114 feet high,

it demonstrated to what extent the railways could disregard natural difficulties. Cropsey assumed a high vantage point to show the vast spaces mastered by the locomotive, at the same time snuggling it benignly into the middle reaches of the landscape. All the old ingredients are present, but now the magisterial gaze is controlled by the railway as it guides the eye down from the primitive hilltop to the dwellings below and thence across the wide valley of promise toward Lanesboro, Pennsylvania.

The peaceful assimilation of technology to the landscape—a picture at odds with what everyone knew in their hearts—is deftly treated in the famous *Lackawanna Valley* by George Inness (Fig. 36).[171] It is the paradigm of the materialization of the magisterial gaze. Inness asserted that he preferred "civilized landscape"—landscape subjugated by human endeavor as opposed to wilderness landscape—but the contrast he draws between the wilder

Fig. 36. George Inness, *The
Lackawanna Valley*, ca. 1855.
National Gallery of Art,
Washington, D.C. Gift of
Mrs. Huttleston Rogers,
1945.

zone on the hilltop and the pollution and ugliness of the roundhouse and sidings below suggests his ambivalence. He elides the rude thicket in depicting the descending slope from the pastoral to the industrial, but he emphasizes the clearing as the eye moves downward by the pervasive presence of the tree stumps strewn across it. The insistent stumps almost parody the "woodsman spare that tree" theme while providing the transition to the valley at the foot of the hill, a view of the growing industrial town of Scranton, Pennsylvania, and the complex of the Delaware, Lackawanna, and Western Railroad Company that commissioned the picture.

The company had been incorporated in 1851 and lost no time in gaining the authorization of the New York and Pennsylvania state legislatures to survey, lay out, and construct their lines, even if that required encroaching on the lands and waters of individuals, including Native Americans.[172] For the purposes of cuttings and embankments the corporation had the right to go beyond the allowable width of the road, taking as much land "as may be necessary for the proper construction and security of the road, and to cut down any standing trees that may be in danger of falling on the road."[173] Although that passage referred to New York State, we may infer that the company received similar authorization in Pennsylvania, which probably explains the standing stumps on the hill overlooking the road in Inness's picture. Here the progress signified by the magisterial gaze specifically implied the power of the railroad to consume the land.

The concept of a transcontinental railroad occupied the forefront of the imagination of the shrewdest land speculators. They understood the connection between expansionism and speculation and attempted to gain possession of the leading sites of future cities. By stimulating and guiding the tide of migration through advocacy of a transcontinental railway, they prospered by the rise of prices of their extensive landholdings in the strategic locations.

Thus did the magisterial gaze get converted into the diagonal of a line of tracks and speeding locomotive carrying civilization to the farthest reaches of the continent. Even as the first emigrant wagon trains were winding their way across the Western landscape, Eastern merchants were avidly promoting the idea of a transcontinental railroad. The idea had already been voiced as early as the 1830s, but it was not until 1844 that Asa Whitney, a New York merchant and railroad promoter grown rich through trade with Asia, presented to Congress a formal proposal for such a rail line. Under his plan, Congress would set aside a sixty-mile-wide tract of land stretching from Lake Michigan to the mouth of the Columbia River, and profits derived from the sale and settlement of this tract would subsidize construction of the railroad.[174]

Although the plan never materialized, it aroused the aspirations of two preeminent agents of Manifest Destiny, Thomas Hart Benton, senator from Missouri, and his son-in-law John Charles Frémont, the most energetic surveyor of the American West in the nineteenth century and seasoned veteran of mountain exploration.[175] Frémont had previously resigned from the Army's Corps of Topographical Engineers—the arm of the federal government responsible for exploration of the West—as a result of a power struggle within the Army in California and his consequent court martial. Nevertheless, he remained the favorite of the expansionists for such dramatic gestures as planting American flags on the summits of the tallest peaks of the Rockies.[176] Financed by wealthy St. Louis interests organized by Benton,[177] Frémont set out in October 1848 to explore the thirty-eighth parallel, a route that once again took him over the formidable Rockies but appeared to be a direct course between St. Louis and San Francisco. Frémont had actually surveyed a railroad line before he left the Topographical Corps, so he could justifiably claim to be conducting the first expert survey of a railroad route to the Pacific.[178] But the expedition quickly turned disastrous, as winter storms and the high altitudes took their toll of the men and animals. Nevertheless, Frémont—one of the fortunate survivors—was now convinced "that neither the snow of winter nor the mountain ranges were obstacles in the way of a [rail]road."[179]

The railroad expeditions launched by the Pacific Railroad Survey Act of 1853—a crash program designed by Congress to determine the most practical and economical route to the Pacific—stimulated collaborative ventures involving a host of specialists of every stripe.[180]

They set out to gather data on the climate, soil, rocks, minerals, and natural history of each route, as well as to evaluate engineering obstacles, economic potential, and the availability of such necessities as timber and water. Like a colonialist expedition, each survey team, led by a topographical engineer, included geographers, botanists, geologists, astronomers, meteorologists, cartographers, and artists, as well as the usual military escort, guide, interpreters, teamsters, carpenters, and blacksmiths. The participating landscape artists—often including second-generation Hudson River painters who owned shares of railroad securities—found themselves in the vanguard of scientific and technical observation on behalf of Manifest Destiny. It is not surprising to learn that the magisterial gaze now comprehended this more sophisticated understanding.

The ability to cut through the mountains and build bridges across rivers gave added as-

Fig. 37. Fanny Frances Palmer, *Across the Continent: "Westward the Course of Empire Takes Its Way,"* 1868. Colored lithograph, published by Currier and Ives. Museum of the City of New York, New York. Harry T. Peters Collection.

surance to the penetrating visual gaze. Fanny Palmer's famous Currier and Ives print, *Across the Continent: "Westward the Course of Empire Takes Its Way,"* executed the year before the completion of the transcontinental railroad, aligns the angle of vision with the limitless track receding precipitously to the farthest reaches of the horizon (Fig. 37). Moving from right to left as it descends a hill to the valley below, it bisects the composition diagonally into a right and wrong side of the tracks. On the left, a village is being built alongside the railroad line; men continue to clear the woods in the hills, children enter a schoolhouse, others run to greet the onrushing train, and in the background a wagon train parallels the tracks as settlers follow the route opened up by the railroad expeditions. On the right, however, two Indians on horseback are stopped by the screen of smoke issuing from the locomotive's smokestack.

As the expeditions and settlers tramped westward, it was inevitable that they would encounter hostile Native Americans from whom they wrested hunting grounds and sacred sites. Now it was no longer a case of mere nostalgia for a vanishing race unable to cope with the onrush of civilization but rather the need to systematically suppress well-organized, determined peoples who resisted the encroachment of the Anglo-Saxons. Anticipating Theodore Roosevelt's myth of the winning of the West, the magisterial gaze no longer begins with the wilderness trace but now tracks the Indians on the run or walled off from their view of the landscape. Those who held "title" to the lands in perpetuity long before the white man arrived are no longer considered entitled to them. This attains absurd proportions in the popular print after John Gast's painting *American Progress,* which, strictly speaking, is not an example of the magisterial gaze but conveys all the ingre-

132

Fig. 38. John Gast, *American Progress,* engraving, 1878.

dients associated with it in schematic fashion (Fig. 38). The view, taken from an impossible height, traces a route from the Eastern Seaboard to the Western prairies. The personification of American Progress, bearing on her forehead the Star of Empire, floats high overhead and leads the parade westward, stringing telegraph wire across the Great Plains and bringing the light of civilization to the dark wastes of the far West, symbolized by the fleeing Indians and buffalo who are dispelled by the "presence of the wondrous vision." The work exemplifies "all those gigantic results of American brains and hands, which have caused the mighty wilderness to blossom like the rose." [181]

Written by George A. Crofutt, whose popular *New Overland Tourist and Pacific Coast Guide* was underwritten by the Union, Central and Southern Pacific Railroad Companies, those words express the hype of the promoters of railroad ventures for profit, who carried along the landscape artists not just for the ride. Landscapists such as Thomas Moran and Albert Bierstadt complied by painting glorious vistas of the West that attracted the investors and tourists of the East when the pictures were exhibited in spectacular and highly publicized circumstances. A pamphlet written for the exhibition of Bierstadt's *Rocky Mountains* stated the by-now stereotyped version of the magisterial gaze: "Upon that very plain where an Indian village stands, a city, populated by our descendants, may rise, and in its art galleries this picture may eventually find a resting place." [182]

Bierstadt had joined his friend author Fitz-Hugh Ludlow on a Western tour by way of the Overland Mail Route in 1863. Ludlow described their experiences in his book *The Heart of the Continent* (1870), originally serialized in *Atlantic Monthly* in 1863. [183] Ludlow wrote a lengthy description of their first sight of Yosemite Valley from Inspiration Point, a verbal

Fig. 39. Albert Bierstadt, *Domes of the Yosemite*, 1867. St. Johnsbury Athenaeum, St. Johnsbury, Vermont. (See color plate.)

transcription of Bierstadt's spectacular outsized *Domes of the Yosemite* (Fig. 39).[184] Both in the painting and in the text the onlooker is methodically guided into receding space created by overlapping foreground to background planes. Their common strategy, to lead the beholder progressively downward from the foreground ledge into the valley, was paralleled by their actual journey into Yosemite Valley. After scanning the panoramic vista from Inspiration Point, they descended into the valley and traced the path of their magisterial gaze.

Bierstadt's ingenious entrepreneurial schemes could match those of the robber barons move for move, and railroad patronage was eminently suited to his talents. During the peak of his fame, he owned major real estate holdings throughout the country. His model was Bayard Taylor, who inspired him to travel west during a lecture stop at New Bedford,

Massachusetts.[185] With his finger on the American pulse, he could even name a newly discovered peak, Mount Corcoran, after one patron whom he likened to the mountain for its "lofty serenity and the firmness of its foundations."[186] From elevated outcroppings, Bierstadt delighted in capturing sweeping views of the valleys reminiscent of the Hudson River imagery. Like his rival Church, he had built a magnificent villa overlooking the Hudson River where he could view breathtaking scenery from strategically located picture windows.[187] In 1871 Bierstadt was commissioned by Collis P. Huntington of the Central Pacific Railroad to do a landscape view along the route of his railway. The painter produced *Donner Lake from the Summit,* showing the Central Pacific train winding its way down from the summit of a particularly rugged stretch of the Sierra Nevadas, one of the last remaining for-

Fig. 40. Albert Bierstadt, *Donner Lake from the Summit*, 1872. Courtesy of The New York Historical Society, New York City.

midable barriers to the immigrants pushing westward (Fig. 40). Episodes of great suffering had stamped the area of Donner Pass with an almost mythic character, and the construction of a railway through it exemplified the triumph of the new machine power.[188] Bierstadt takes us from the storm-blasted tree trunks of the proverbial wilderness zone down toward the luminous lake in the distance, as if to suggest that now it is the railway that carries us to a brighter future.

MONARCH OF ALL YOU SURVEY

The term "survey" has been used throughout this essay as both metaphor of vigilance and explanation of material practice. In this final section, I want to take up the question of the relation of practical surveying to the magisterial gaze. As in the case of Bayard Taylor, the tension between fixing one's own boundary as a

sign of possession of the land and the urge to transcend boundaries centered on the surveyor of the locality and the surveyor of the nation. Land speculation and settlement, and above all the Western expeditions and explorations, depended first of all on the leadership of the surveyor. Lewis and Clark, Boone, Frémont, John Wesley Powell, F. V. Hayden, and Clarence King were surveyors, and they gave their names to the major expeditions for the overland routes. The charting of uncharted areas, the systematic mapping of the continent, is first and foremost the surveyor's actualization of the magisterial gaze. All the conflicts over boundaries—regional, national, and international—masked by the rhetoric and bombast of Manifest Destiny are expressed in the surveyor's language of the lines of longitude and latitude.

It is through surveying that the particular configuration of the American cultural system shaped spatial processes and structures in the nation. Its prime function in setting boundaries and fixing locations has molded the visible and invisible features of the landscape. It is the material means by which Americans gained control over space as well as over their individual habitats. The apotheosis of the frontiersman triumphantly carving an autonomous barony out of the wilderness is intimately connected with the surveyor's instruments. Although no pioneer, even George Washington, the putative father of our country, participated in the myth as the youthful surveyor of Alexandria, Virginia.

The remorseless dividing up of the continent following the authorization by Congress of the Land Ordinance of 1785 (which determined the spatial organization of two thirds of the nation) only fueled the dream of an indefinite projection westward.[189] Surveying itself took on an obsessional character on the local level,

but in the context of the dream it spun an invisible web of lines over the surface of the continent. In this sense, the world becomes a mechanical system subject to human control and expressed in quantifiable terms. Thus the imposing of order on an unruly wilderness required the work of the surveyor in a practical role and as purveyor of the myth of the infinite extension of the land. The tramp of the pioneers westward meant that the land had to be locally exploited—worked, cubed, and sold—as quickly as possible and that the process should continue indefinitely as they moved on to establish the next settlement. That is the heart of the curious paradox in American history of the juxtaposition of the vulgar material obsession with real estate and the visionary and utopian fantasy of a new world order under American influence. The magisterial gaze answers to this expansionist fantasy by always projecting the vision across the valley as a step ahead of the point where the viewer is located at any given time; hence the tension between the edge of the wilderness coulisse and the Edenic setting within the gaze, the metaphor for the dynamic progress from a primitive set of conditions to an increasingly complex civilized existence. The nineteenth-century American landscapist projected the topographical amalgamation of pastoral scene, cityscape, and interface areas.

It is the rectilinear survey that objectified the American dream, but in also delimiting the dream, it aroused the fury of those who hated boundaries and straight lines. Settlers in the backlands who needed markets could admire the surveyors and engineers of turnpikes, canals, and railroads that existed beyond the locality and fulfilled the vision of continental nationhood. The surveyor, the real estate speculator, and the agents of Manifest Destiny worked hand in hand, when they were not

aspects of one and the same person. The pre-eminent explorer of the West, John C. Frémont, joined these talents to his work for other like-minded types, including his father-in-law, Thomas Hart Benton. Frémont's wife, Jessie Benton, summed up her husband's exploits: "Railroads followed the lines of his journeyings—a nation followed his maps to their resting place—and cities have risen on the ashes of his lonely campfires." [190]

Frémont's surveying skills played a role in the government's Indian strategy, especially in the territory occupied by the Cherokee Indians. Because the Cherokees militantly opposed the federal government's policy of transferring the major tribes to areas west of the Mississippi River, the War Department concluded that a survey would aid military purposes if a war broke out, or if not, at least facilitate the distribution of land among the settlers. It was that early commission that shaped Frémont's career, for according to his own testimony, "the occupation of my prime of life was to be among Indians and waste places." [191]

Surveying and Indian policy became a fundamental function of the U.S. Corps of Topographical Engineers. While later surveyors felt more ambivalent than Frémont (who condoned Kit Carson's murderous assault on Native Americans), they justified the extermination of the Indians on practical and economic grounds. George Wheeler, who headed the U.S. Geographical Surveys West of the One-Hundredth Meridian, interrupts his survey reports with a didactic lesson on the Indian problem. In his 1879 report he notes that the government's "peace-at-any-cost policy" has only encouraged "these red-skinned assassins":

> Unfortunately, the bones of murdered citizens cannot rise to cry out and attest the atrocious murders of the far-spreading and wide-extending border lands of the Great West, and while the fate of the Indian is sealed, the interval during which their extermination as a race is to be consummated will doubtless be marked in addition to Indian outbreaks, with still many more murderous ambuscades and massacres. [192]

Commissioned to make regular reports on the topography and land distribution of Indian reservations, Wheeler observed in a later report that immigration of white settlers was becoming irrepressible in these zones:

> The ever restless surging tide of population, almost a law unto itself, already in many cases crowd over the borders of these reservations, and the time is not far distant when the question of the surrender of these lands to actual settlers will naturally be answered in the affirmative, on the plea of the greatest good for the greatest number. [193]

Wheeler admits that great crimes have been committed against the indigenous peoples, but this has to be understood in the larger, practical scheme of things:

The history, yet to be written, of the contact of American civilization with the aboriginals, the subjugation of the latter, the expropriation of the lands, through conquest and "treaty," the gradual apparent decimation of these races, their amalgamation in part, and the hastening of their final extinction, furnish food for the ethnologist and philosopher, but scarcely for the practical man of affairs, intent on wresting from productive nature the largest bounty, through whose agency treaties have doubtless too often been made for Indians to misunderstand, and which the government has been prevented from enforcing.

In language reminiscent of the landscapist's representation of despairing Native Americans before the onslaught of civilization, Wheeler continues:

It is not at all strange that this child of wonder and fear, viewing nature and man more through the external senses, should resist the approach of civilization that apparently despoils him of most that life holds dear. This resistance, always a forlorn hope, has had its day for the Indians of the Western mountains. Their warlike spirit is now broken, and these hardy sons of nature are now gradually adopting the ways of peace and civilization. The result of this control, assimilation, and gradual absorption, can better be seen a century hence from now.[194]

In the end, however, the Indian is essentially a "creature of impulse that can only be controlled through fear," and hence a perpetual military presence is necessary "to preserve and defend both the interests of the white man and Indian." Here is the fork-tongued lingo of the surveyor for whom control of the populations of the West is the moral and political equivalent of imposing order on the surface of the land.

Clarence King, who organized the U.S. Geological Survey and became its first director, was more sanguine in regard to the indigenous peoples. He declared that "any policy toward the Indians based upon the assumption of their being brutes or devils was nothing short of a blot on this Christian century." [195] Yet he could deride the Native American "genius for loafing," as well as the California "greasers" whose indolence and conniving ways ran counter to his sense of national purpose. [196]

King and Wheeler were younger rivals of Ferdinand V. Hayden, the most renowned geologist-surveyor of the West. [197] Hayden began his career as the partner of an Indian agent, working on speculation in the field of natural-history collecting. The Indian agent would pay Hayden's expenses for a year's collecting in the Dakotas, and they would share the profits from selling complete sets of specimens to wealthy collectors and universities. It meant trespassing on Sioux territory in the northern Great Plains—where the surveyors regularly accompanied expeditions to suppress the Indians—and stealing their animal, mineral, and fossil wealth for fun and profit. At no time did the surveyor-chiefs of expeditions ever separate their commercial motives from scientific pursuits, and that meant engaging in perpetual hostilities with the Native Americans.

As a result of Hayden's expertise, he was assigned in 1856 to a government survey of the Dakotas to supply valuable information on the Sioux country. Hayden's gift for public relations and ambition made him one of the most popular of the surveyors. He never failed to advertise the progress of Western settlement and tied it to his own expeditions. In his reports he rarely failed to point out to his readers "some of the pioneers whose labors have done much toward calling the attention of the world to this great West."[198] Later, when he published *The Great West: Its Attractions and Resources,* his publisher reminded the public of Hayden's fundamental role in opening up this "formerly unknown land to the settler." Indeed, thanks to Hayden,

> The rapidity with which the far Western portion of our country has been explored and mapped, and the extraordinary changes made by bringing the vast plains—but lately the roving grounds of wild Indians and herds of buffaloes—into cultivation, furnishing flourishing and happy homes for hundreds of thousands of the restless population of the East or

of Europe . . . have excited the astonishment of the world.[199]

Hayden never lost an opportunity for fusing his scientific pursuits with his entrepreneurial interests, as in the case of his exploration of William Gilpin's immense tract of land in Colorado. Gilpin, perhaps the foremost nineteenth-century theorist of Manifest Destiny, owned nearly one million acres of Colorado real estate.[200] Planning to put it on the market, he called in specialists to survey his empire for its mineral and agricultural potential. An English speculator interested in the land hired Hayden to report on the estate, and Hayden concluded that he knew "of no region of the West more desirable of settlement" and that "rich returns of gold" had yet to be made. Hayden received for his assistance in land promotion $10,000 worth of stock. Although Hayden's biographers dispute the suggestion of a conflict of interest, Hayden had a habit of finding something positive to say about every region he surveyed, even when his enthusiasm was not well founded.[201] But that attitude assured his popularity among the Western speculators, who willingly supported his regular requests for grants to continue his surveys.

Hayden was criticized, however, for attempting to cover vast amounts of territory rapidly and superficially to gain credit for as many discoveries as possible. One critic advised Hayden not to exaggerate the novelty of his work, that he need not be "monarch of all he surveys." Respecting the real value of his achievements, the critic reminded the surveyor that "the whole boundless continent ain't his'n."[202] Yet that was precisely the attitude that all the surveyors shared with each other and with the expansionists of every stripe.

Gilpin, working closely with the surveyors, eventually became a millionaire and Denver socialite. Gilpin had been involved in land speculation and real estate deals almost all of his adult life and was closely connected with the circles around Thomas Hart Benton and Frémont.[203] Gilpin joined Frémont's second expedition to Oregon.[204] Later, Gilpin created a vast development scheme near Independence, Missouri, which his contemporaries called Gilpintown. He conceived of a colossal city, Centropolis, that would fuse Independence, Kansas City, and Westport into the hub of a transcontinental railway and become the largest urban center in the nation.[205] He confessed to learning a lesson or two from Tocqueville (who visited Gilpin's brother Henry in 1831) on how to read "the future with a good deal of reliability from the data the present affords."[206]

The real estate magnate and railroad promoter was the theorist who declared "Progress is God" and announced a program for the American people informed with a vision of power, unity, and unceasing forward motion.[207] An ardent antisocialist, racist, and jingoist who wanted to annex Mexico and Canada, he defined the American people narrowly as those of northern European stock. In his vision, he could see in this group "a new power, *the People occupied in the wilderness,* engaged at once in extracting from its recesses the omnipotent element of *gold coin,* and disbursing it immediately for the *industrial* conquest of the world."[208]

This was his view from the summit of the Rocky Mountains, the immense mountain formation of North America filling out the space of the continent to the Pacific. Taking this cue from Humboldt's *Cosmos,* Gilpin perceived the great progress of the world along an axis of the "isothermal temperate zone." This is the line of the advance of civilization, radiating intelligence, and toward it "all people have struggled to converge."[209] Gilpin's theoretical model often invokes the surveyor's terminology, lines of convergence, baselines, meridians. His theory follows the trajectory of the magisterial gaze when he proclaims his favorite motto: "Behold the sublime panorama which crowns the middle region of our Union, fans the fire of patriotism, and beckons on the energetic host of our people."[210]

The South Pass through which he wants to run his continental railway is the "*continental line,*" that line along which empire runs "with unerring certainty." In fact, for Gilpin the railroad itself is transcendent, "more powerful and more permanent than law, or popular consent, or political constitutions."[211] Thus does he translate the magisterial gaze into the abstract lines of the surveyor traversing the continent. As he states,

A glance of the eye, thrown across the North American continent, accompanying the course of the sun from ocean to ocean, reveals an extraordinary landscape. It displays immense forces, characterized by order, activity, and progress. The structure of nature—the marching of a vast population—the creations of the people, individually and combined—are seen in infinite varieties of form and gigantic dimensions. Farms, cities, States, public works, define themselves, flash into form, accumulate, combine, and harmonize. The pioneer army perpetually advances, reconnoitres, strikes to the front. Empire plants itself on the trails.[212]

Here is a marvelous text to complement the visual properties of the magisterial gaze; it has the evangelical fervor of Benton, who declaimed, "Pierce the Rocky Mountains, and hew their highest crag into a statue of Columbus, pointing the old world on the way to the Indies!"[213] Or again, the rhetoric of Gilpin's admirer, the Protestant minister Thomas Starr King, who assumed the same cosmic prospect to exemplify the aesthetics of eminent domain:

Suppose that the continent could turn towards you to-morrow at sunrise, and show to you the whole American area in the short hours of the sun's advance from Eastport to the Pacific! You would see New England roll into light from the green plumes of Aroostook to the silver stripe of the Hudson; westward thence over the Empire State, and over the lakes, and over the sweet valleys of Pennsylvania, and over the prairies, the morning blush would run and waken all the line of the Mississippi; . . . beyond this line another basin, too, the Missouri, catching the morning sun, leads your eye along its western slope, till the Rocky Mountains burst upon the vision, and yet do not bar it; across its passes we must follow, as the stubborn courage of American pioneers has forced its way, till again the Sierra and their silver veins are tinted along the mighty bulwark with the break of day; and then over to the gold-fields of the western slope, and the fatness of the California soil, and the beautiful valleys of Oregon, and the stately forests of Washington, the eye is drawn, as the globe turns out of the night-shadow, and when the Pacific waves are crested with radiance, you have the one blending picture, nay, the reality, of the American domain![214]

What needs to be emphasized here are the links of continuity between the Knickerbocker and Hudson River attitudes and those of the Western trailblazers (who are often one and the same). Starr King was a transplanted New Englander who took over the Unitarian Society in San Francisco in 1860; in Boston he promoted New England scenery as energetically as he would the Western landscape. His most important work is a description of the scenery of the White Mountains and surroundings in which he quotes Bryant, Willis, and Taylor and makes allusions of familiarity to the Hudson River artists. He espies a motif "such as Ken-

sett loves to paint," and as he prepares to end his excursion he asks rhetorically, "Is one visit enough to satisfy a man of taste with a collection that has three or four first-rate pictures, each by a Church, a Durand, a Bierstadt, a Gignoux?"[215]

Similarly, when Gilpin is on a roll he sounds exactly like Thomas Cole: "Behold, then, rising now and in the future, the empire which industry and self-government create. The growth of half a century, hewed out of the wilderness—its weapons, the axe and plow; its tactics, labor and energy; its soldiers, free and equal citizens."[216] Finally, gazing down from the Rockies on the site of the nascent town of Denver, Gilpin demonstrates that the magisterial gaze moved westward with the surveyors:

There is an intoxicating grandeur in the panorama which unveils itself to the spectator looking out from the crest of our neighboring

Cordillera. In front, in rear, and on either flank, nature ascends to the highest standard of excellence. Behold to the right the Mississippi Basin; to the left the Plateau of the Table Lands; beneath, the family of Parks; around, the radiating backs of the primeval mountains; . . . a chequered landscape, from which no element of sublimity is left out—fertility and food upon the surface; metals beneath; uninterrupted facility of transit. Behold here the panorama which crowns the middle region of our union, fans the immortal fire of patriotism, and beckons on the energetic host of our people.[217]

The surveyors all employed the same high-flown philosophical and aesthetic lingo for rationalizing national conquest and the subjugation of the Native American population. In language reminiscent of Leutze's mural inscription, Frémont wrote in his *Memoirs,* "Shut in to narrow limits, the mind is driven in upon itself

and loses it's elasticity; but the breast expands when, upon some hill-top, the eye ranges over a broad expanse of country, or in the face of an ocean. We do not value enough the effect of space for the eye; it reacts upon the mind, which unconsciously expands to larger limits and freer range of thoughts."[218]

Typical of the Easterner, Clarence King (who lived near the Hudson River) also masked his driving purpose in terms of the magisterial gaze: "There is a grandeur, a spaciousness which expand and fit the mind for yet larger sensations when you shall stand on the height above."[219] As he climbs Mount Shasta, what urges him on is precisely this expectation of immensity: "I think such vastness of prospect now and then extremely valuable in itself; it forcibly widens one's conception of country, driving away such false notion of extent or narrowing idea of limitation as we get in living on lower plains."[220] This enlarged prospect is inextricably tied to the sense of expansion: "I never tire of overlooking these great wide fields, studying their rich variety, and giving myself up to the expansion which is the instant and lasting reward. In presence of these vast spaces and all but unbounded outlook, the hours hurry by with singular swiftness." King's panoramic vision is then connected with the national purpose: "Before quitting the ridge, Fred Clark and I climbed together out upon the highest pinnacle, a trachyte needle rising a few feet above the rest, and so small we could barely balance there together, but we stood there a moment and waved the American flag, looking down over our shoulders eleven thousand feet." [221]

This confounding of the patriotic duty with personal vision also reveals itself in Frémont's daring planting of the flag at the summit of one of the highest peaks in the Rocky Mountains. Just at that moment a bee landed on the site, and the party could not help analogizing their expedition with the insect's triumph: "We pleased ourselves with the idea that he was the first of his species to cross the mountain barrier, a solitary pioneer to foretell the advance of civilization." [222] Hence the growing self-consciousness of the westward movement in relation to the magisterial gaze. And for all, including King, the tough-minded scientist, God-Nature sanctioned this advance.

The surveyors shared the vision of the businessman Nathaniel Langford, who financed a survey of the country that is now Yellowstone National Park. Although he would later spearhead the movement to establish the national park, he nevertheless envisioned its settlement by a privileged elite:

How can I sum up its wonderful attractions! It is dotted with islands of great beauty, as yet unvisited by man, but which at no remote period will be adorned with villas and the ornaments of civilized life. . . . It possesses adaptabilities for the highest display of artificial culture, and the greatest wonders of Nature that the world affords, and is beautified by the grandeur of the most extensive mountain scenery, and not many years can elapse before the march of civil improvement will reclaim this delightful solitude, and garnish it with all the attractions of cultivated taste and refinement.[223]

Naturally, that vision made him feel "as never before my entire dependence upon that Almighty Power who had wrought these wonders."

Thus the surveyors and their sponsors, the scientists and the magnates, were one on the question of Manifest Destiny. It is no coincidence that the organized expeditions were known as surveys, since the goals were basically to monitor the area under exploration as well as to map it. The mapping of vast, uncharted lands with regard to direction and distance depends on the geometric proposition that the intersection of two lines is a point. It is the intersection of longitude and latitude that determines location, the starting point of the survey. The major surveys, those that covered large expanses of land, depended on the practice of triangulation. This method was taught in basic civil engineering courses and recommended as the most accurate form of surveying.[224] Triangulation is based on the trigonometric proposition that if the length of one side and three angles of a triangle are known, the length of the other two sides can be calculated without measuring. In addition, if the direction of one side is known, the directions of the remaining sides can be determined.[225]

Practiced in surveying for centuries, it was not until the late eighteenth century, with the invention of the theodolite, that it could be systematically applied for mapping over long distances. Triangulation was made to order for large, extensive areas, and its success depended on high vantage points so that the line of sight was clear of all obstructions. It proved especially advantageous in mountainous regions such as the Appalachians, the Hudson River Valley, the hill country of New England, and, of course, the Western mountain ranges, where the peaks and summits furnished natural points for stations.[226] Triangulation worked best when the stations had commanding views of the surrounding country.[227] Both Ferdinand Hayden and Clarence King used lightweight theodolites for observations from mountain peak to mountain peak as part of the triangulation process. This enabled their topographers to concentrate on the mountain ranges and cover relatively large areas in a short time. One of the most stunning photographs by Hayden's photographer, William H. Jackson, shows triangulation operations on the summit of Silverton

Mountain in Colorado (Fig. 41). Indeed, the photographers often climbed out on the highest vantage points to take shots of the valley below in emulation of the magisterial gaze they had experienced in the work of the landscapists (Fig. 42).

Topographical charting and mapping related directly to landscape painting, except that in the latter the ideology was masked by the aesthetics of the magisterial gaze. While the sketches by the surveyors, or by artists hired by the surveyors, served to illustrate scientific and factual reports, in so far as they participated in the trailblazing process and plotted the terrain for the settlers they may be considered practical translations of the landscapist's projections. Both the surveyor and the landscapist regarded the wilderness as simply a stage in the civilizing process, a place to be settled and developed in the future.

The curriculum of the West Point Mili-

Fig. 41. William H. Jackson, *Triangulation Operations on Silverton Mountain,* photograph, 1874. National Archives and Records Administration, Washington, D.C.

Fig. 42. William H. Jackson, *Mount Harvard and the Valley of the Arkansas,* photograph, ca. 1875. National Archives and Records Administration, Washington, D.C.

tary Academy provided a direct link between the topographical drawing of the surveyor and the Hudson River school. Located on the Hudson, its students were taught to draw scenic views in the area, and inevitably their work resembled the work of the painters. Robert W. Weir, a painter in touch with the members of the Hudson River school and a teacher of topographical drawing at West Point, taught his students to sketch the environment around them. One pupil of the academy who frequently sketched the Hudson scenery, J. B. Abert, became a prominent topographer for Western surveys and mapped New Mexico for the U.S. Army.[228]

Often the topographical draftsman and the fine artist were one and the same, as in the case of John Mix Stanley. Born in New York, Stanley was the most celebrated of the artists who traveled in an official capacity with the Pacific Railroad Surveys.[229] His painting *Scouts in*

the Tetons assumes an elevated point of view identical to that of the scouts who survey the landscape, and it agrees most remarkably with a topographical draftsman's sketch of a triangulation station in the valley of the Great Salt Lake (Figs. 43, 44). Here we see most dramatically the connection between the painter's conception of the magisterial view and the practical application of the surveyor's methods.

Survey triangulation aims at the large-scale picture, constructing a vast geometrical framework of triangles before filling in local topographical detail. Maps showing triangulation surveys often indicate a network of diagonals radiating outward from high stations (Fig. 45). This method began by fixing points at the map's outer limits and then filled in lines of routes and other details. In that sense, its directional azimuths may be likened to the unlimited penetration of the magisterial gaze. The clumps of trees on the summits or level

Fig. 43. Sketch of triangulation station for Stansbury Expedition, 1849. Denver Public Library, Western History Department.

Fig. 44. John Mix Stanley,
Scouts in the Tetons, 1860.
Thomas Gilcrease Institute of
American History and Art,
Tulsa, Oklahoma. (See color
plate.)

plateaus of hills in so many nineteenth-century American landscapes are not necessarily the stereotyped coulisse but the points of reference for the surveyor's sighting.[230] The church or a significant house in the valley also becomes a signal for the surveyor, helping to establish the baseline and fix on the grid of the continent. Theoretically, you can triangulate to infinity and thus establish unity out of infinity—the principle behind the magisterial gaze and the practical realization of Manifest Destiny. As a youthful Asher B. Durand declaimed in a Fourth of July oration at the Springfield Pres-byterian Church,

> When we contemplate the astonishing progress of this Republic along the plane of continued elevation, when we survey the splendid struc-ture of our Federal Government, the rapidity of our improvement in Agriculture, Literature, and the Arts, together with the glorious achievements of our Immortal Heroes, and

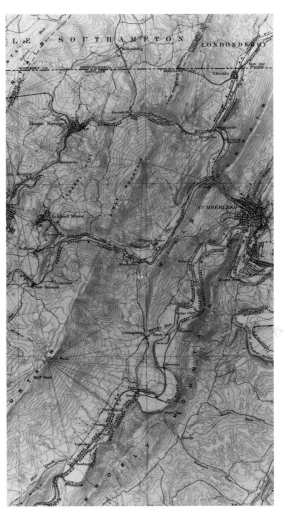

Fig. 45. Diagram of triangu-lation, 1898.

when in contact with which we see all Nature
conspiring, subservient to advance us to the
highest pinnacles of glory—have we not cause
to look up to Heaven with eternal gratitude?
Have we not reason to exclaim, Happy
America![231]

Durand's peroration showed that no responsible
and enlightened citizen of the time was likely
to forget that geography—celestial as well as
terrestrial—was the necessary first step to economic penetration and ultimately to political
domination.

MOUNT RUSHMORE:
AN EXCURSUS

Gutzon Borglum recorded his feelings when he
stood for the first time on the crest of Mount
Rushmore, towering 6,200 feet above sea level:
"I was conscious we were in another world . . .
and there a new thought seized me—a thought
that was to redirect me and dominate all my
carving—the scale of that mountain peak." He
then continued: "We looked out over a horizon
level and beaten like the rim of a great cart-
wheel 2,000 feet below. We had reached upward toward the heavenly bodies . . . and it
came over me in an almost terrifying manner
that I had never sensed what I was planning.
Plans must change. The vastness here de-
manded it."[232] Thus Mount Rushmore crystal-
lizes the magisterial gaze into rock hardness
through monstrous omniscient heads looming
over the Western landscape. Borglum's staring
effigies are in fact surrogates for the sculptor
himself surveying the endless tracts of land and
consuming them with his gaze (Fig. 46).

The son of Danish immigrant parents who
settled in the West, Borglum internalized the
fierce chauvinism of first-generation American
parents. His maturation coincided with the
consummation of the new industrial order of

Fig. 46. Mount Rushmore, completed in 1941. Keystone, South Dakota. Courtesy of the South Dakota Department of Tourism.

America and with the transition of the imaginative ideal of the pioneer charting new worlds in the wilderness to the postbellum myth of enterprising captains of industry restructuring the world through their inventive genius and daring. Borglum's contribution to American culture may be seen as an expression of his need to combine both mythological ideals in his life and work. He lived out the Western fantasy of rugged individualism and dominion over larger and larger units of land, but he accomplished his goals with modern technology and a team of subordinates. He carved a granitic mountain as a piece of sculpture with pneumatic jackhammers and plugs of dynamite.

From the start, Borglum considered Mount Rushmore a site for tourism, not however in its natural state, like a Niagara Falls or a Yellowstone National Park, but in its altered state wrought by human artifice. It impresses

not through the wild grandeur of its local geography but through the triumph of modern culture over that geography. Here the contest between nature and culture took the form of a pitched battle. Borglum and his associates wrenched away thousands of tons of rock to re-represent the original mountain in anthropomorphic guise. God-created Man now recreates Nature in his own image, realizing through technology the fantasy of the artist usurping the divine prerogative.

Borglum's theme for Mount Rushmore was "the founding, preservation, growth, and development of the nation,"[233] a hymn to Manifest Destiny. Seeking information on Thomas Jefferson from George Gordon Battle at the outset of his Mount Rushmore commission, Borglum stated, "Jefferson's place in this memorial is more important even than Washington's. By that I do not mean to eclipse

Washington one iota, but Jefferson purchased the Louisiana Territory, in the center of which, on a spur of the Rocky Mountains, this memorial is located. I am literally converting a spur of the Rockies into a memorial and a monument to the great Western Republic." Borglum understood Jefferson's acquisition to be the key to the unfolding of the saga of Manifest Destiny:

> It was the acquisition of the Louisiana Territory that led to the colonization of Texas by Americans and that eventually to the Mexican trouble. It was the struggle over the precise relationship of Texas to the United States that led to the acquisition of California. It was the opening of the Northwest by Lewis and Clark, the direct agents of Jefferson, that developed the Oregon Trail and that, in turn, determined the boundary with Canada. In other words, it was Jefferson's political strategy in securing the Mississippi that incidentally gave us the Continent westward to the Pacific.[234]

Mount Rushmore also metaphorically points to the idea of Manifest Destiny and all the tragedy it brought in its wake for native peoples.

Borglum's initial idea demonstrates that he had cut his teeth on William Gilpin and the rest: "I want somewhere in America on or near the Rockies, the backbone of the Continent, so far removed from succeeding, selfish, coveting civilizations, a few feet of stone that bears witness, carries the likenesses, the dates, a word or two of the great things we accomplished as a Nation, placed so high it won't pay to pull down for lesser purposes."[235] Although not depicting a narrative, Borglum's program for the memorial clearly summarized America's national conquest. His wife, who served as his amanuensis, wrote that the memorial constituted her husband's "sincere patriotic effort to

Fig. 47. Closeup of Abraham Lincoln profile, Mount Rushmore. Courtesy of the South Dakota Department of Tourism.

preserve and perpetuate the ideals of liberty and freedom on which our government was established and to record the territorial expansion of the Republic."[236] His choice of four presidents for the Mount Rushmore memorial testifies to his position as a latecomer on the stage of magisterial aesthetics: each had a role in founding and consummating the myth of America's Manifest Destiny. George Washington, who dominates in projecting out the farthest, extensively surveyed what was then the western wilderness; Thomas Jefferson, deliberately positioned to face west, doubled the nation's landmass with the Louisiana Purchase and commissioned Lewis and Clark to explore the first land route to the Pacific, eventually opening the West to settlement; Abraham Lincoln (Fig. 47), for whom Borglum named his son, preserved the Union; and Theodore Roosevelt, Borglum's favorite, was responsible for the building of the Panama Canal, which fulfilled

Columbus's dream of a water route to the Far East and opened a new access to the West, quickening the industrial development of the nation and consummating its empire. Borglum's plan also included a huge panel in the shape of the Louisiana Purchase, on which would be inscribed in eight-foot-high, five-inch-deep, gilded letters the nine great events in American history, seven of which—after the signing of the Declaration of Independence and the framing of the Constitution—had to do with the acquisition of territory: the Louisiana Purchase, the admission of Texas to the Union, and the acquisition of Florida, California, Oregon, Alaska, and the Panama Canal Zone.

Borglum profoundly admired the Western explorers and entrepreneurs like Thomas Hart Benton and Benton's son-in-law John Charles Frémont. Like them, he imagined himself a lone crusader in the quest to make an enduring monument for the continental republic. It was

Benton who, in an address proposing a transcontinental road in 1849, declared that it would be crowned with a colossal statue of Columbus, "hewn from a granite mass or a peak on the Rocky Mountains, . . . pointing with outstretched arm to the western horizon, and saying to the flying passengers—'There is the East; there is India'."[237] The reviews of an early painting, *Staging Over the Sierra Madre Mountains in California,* brought Borglum to the attention of Frémont's wife, Jessie Benton, who became his most enthusiastic champion. When she persuaded her husband to sit for Borglum, she brought together two generations of American males desiring to transfix the world with their magisterial gaze. When Borglum planted the national flag on Mount Rushmore for the dedication of the mountain in 1925, he was emulating Frémont's dramatic gesture of unfurling the flag at the summit of the Rockies.

Consistent with the pattern of destruction

following in the train of exploration and empire building, the dedication of Mount Rushmore was one more symbolic instance of the white man's racist and intolerant Indian policy. Mount Rushmore stands between the boundaries of Harney National Forest and Custer State Park, two of the most hated names in the Sioux lexicon. Both Harney and Custer engaged in Sioux massacres, including the murder of women and children, and led illegal expeditions into the Black Hills to provoke the Native Americans to hostile confrontation. The Black Hills, of which Mount Rushmore is part, were known as the sacred site of Paha Sapa, holy mountains where ceremonies were held for the spirits of dead warriors and where the young came alone to meditate and pray for guidance from the Great Spirit. Following the bloody Sioux war of 1865–67, the United States negotiated the Fort Laramie Treaty of 1868, which created the Great Sioux Reserva-

tion, encompassing 41,000 square miles of the Black Hills, for the exclusive use of the Dakota Indians. But in 1874 General Custer violated the treaty by leading an army of one thousand troops into the Black Hills on the pretext of surveying a possible fort site. Custer deliberately constructed a glowing official report of the fertility of the lands and possibilities for cattle grazing, and then tacked on near the end the discovery of a gold vein.[238] Rumors of gold induced tens of thousands of prospectors to swarm into the Black Hills, and the half-hearted government, faced with economic depression and high agrarian unemployment, relinquished its commitment to the Sioux. The outraged Sioux and other northern Native Americans reacted violently. Eventually President Grant declared all-out war, compelling the Indians to sue for peace and assemble in barren preserves in Indian territory, to be ravaged by disease and hunger. The military then forced a selection of them to agree to turn over more than seven million acres, including the Black Hills, to the United States government. The last incident of the Indian wars was the sickening Wounded Knee massacre in 1890, in which U.S. troops mowed down two hundred Dakota men, women, and children.

After the wars, the Sioux underwent a different kind of attack, on their society, customs, religion, and tribal unity, as the government tried to integrate them into white civilization. They fought back in the white man's court, trying to get satisfaction for the theft of their land and the violations of the treaties. That process was still going on at the time Borglum planted the American flag on the summit of Mount Rushmore to dedicate the memorial. He then proceeded to desecrate the site by defacing it with the effigies of four great white fathers hewn into the granite to withstand the ravages of erosion for a million years. The harmony that the Native Americans had established with their environment was disrupted in a double sense by Borglum's monument, first through the usurpation of a religious and cultural site and second through its destruction as an integral feature of the indigenous landscape.

It is no wonder that the Sioux Indians came to despise the pale face's monumental impress on their sacred hills, a humiliating symbol of their oppression. As Lame Deer, a Sioux medicine man, interpreted it:

What does this Mount Rushmore mean to us Indians? It means that these big white faces are telling us, "First we gave you Indians a treaty that you could keep these Black Hills forever, as long as the sun would shine, in exchange for all the Dakotas, Wyoming and Montana. Then we found the gold and took this last piece of land, because we were stronger, and there were more of us than there were of you, and because we had cannons and Gatling guns, while you hadn't even progressed far enough to make a steel knife. And when you didn't want to leave, we wiped you out, and those of you who survived we put on reservations. And then we took the gold out, a billion bucks, and we aren't through yet. And because we like the tourist dollars, too, we have made your sacred Black Hills into one vast Disneyland. And after we did all this we carved up this mountain, the dwelling place of your spirits, and put our four gleaming white faces here. We are the conquerors."

Lame Deer noted the psychological impact of the great white heads on the tourists who look up to them "and feel good, real good, because they make them feel big and powerful." They strut and think, "'We are white, and made this, and what we want we get, and nothing can stop us.'" Lame Deer concluded,

> And this is what conquering means. They could just as well have carved this mountain into a huge cavalry boot standing on a dead Indian.

Thus Borglum's memorial constituted the crowning touch to Western expansion and at the same time permanently etched into the landscape the magisterial gaze.

1. See the discussion of Cole in B. J. Wolf, *Romantic Re-Vision* (Chicago: University of Chicago Press, 1982), pp. 186–200.

2. I was at first struck by the coincidence of my theory with the advertising formulae of the twentieth century, and then gradually came to realize that my generation had been inculcated with the message first promulgated by the nineteenth-century elite. See Roland Marchand, *Advertising the American Dream: Making Way for Modernity, 1920–1940* (Berkeley: University of California Press, 1985), pp. 238–57.

3. The pioneering work here has been Barbara Novak, *Nature and Culture: American Landscape and Painting 1825–1875* (New York: Oxford University Press, 1980). See also Katherine Manthorne, *Creation and Renewal: Views of Cotopaxi by Frederic Edwin Church* (Washington, D.C.: National Museum of American Art and Smithsonian Institution Press, 1985), pp. 31–51.

4. One outstanding exception is Alan Wallach, "Thomas Cole and the Aristocracy," *Arts Magazine* 56 (November 1981), pp. 94–106. See also E. Johns, "Art, History, and Curatorial Responsibility," *American Quarterly* 41 (March

1989), pp. 143–54. For the literary analogue to this trope see H. M. Sayre, "Surveying the Vast Profound: The Panoramic Landscape in American Consciousness," *Massachusetts Review* 24 (Winter 1983), pp. 723–42.

5. "The Wisdom of Doc Peets," quoted in Robert Taft, *Artists and Illustrators of the Old West 1850–1900* (New York: Scribner, 1953), p. 239.

6. F. J. Turner, *The Frontier in American History* (New York: Holt, Rinehart and Winston, 1967), p. 11.

7. The base of this research has been the intellectual and cultural histories of H. N. Smith, *The Virgin Land: The American West as Symbol and Myth* (Cambridge, Mass.: Harvard University Press, 1950); R. W. B. Lewis, *The American Adam: Innocence, Tragedy, and Tradition in the Nineteenth Century* (Chicago: University of Chicago Press, 1955); Hans Huth, *Nature and the American: Three Centuries of Changing Attitudes* (Berkeley, University of California Press, 1957); Roderick Nash, *Wilderness and the American Mind* (New Haven: Yale University Press, 1967).

8. The landscapist Jasper Francis Cropsey quoted in Novak, *Nature and Culture*, p. 5.

9. Alexis de Tocqueville, *Journey to America* (New York: Doubleday, 1971), p. 399.

10. Elisée Reclus, *Correspondence*, Vol. I (Paris: Librairie Schleicher Frères, 1911–25), p. 92.

11. T. Cole, "Essay on American Scenery," *American Monthly Magazine*, new series, Vol. 1 (January 1836), p. 12. See also Sarah Burns, *Pastoral Inventions: Rural Life in Nineteenth-Century American Art and Culture* (Philadelphia: Temple University Press, 1989), pp. 12–13.

12. James Fenimore Cooper's "Remarks on the *Course of Empire*" emphasizes the synchronicity of the series from the start: he declares that the first picture shows us "not only what the nation-hero is doing at the moment we gaze upon him, but also what he has *been* doing, and yet *will* do." And a little later, he elaborates by asserting that "the empire appears, not at its birth, nor at its transition to youth, but at a period which suggests them both. Speeding past us, a creature of new life, it is arrested at a moment vividly expressive of its total childhood." More significant, in the central picture of empire at its peak, "in the all-possessing effulgence of the present, we both have a sense of the past and divine the future." See L. L. Noble, *The Life and Works of Thomas Cole, N.A.* (New York: Sheldon and Co., 1860), pp. 169–72. For an excellent reappraisal of the series and its political encoding see A. Miller, "Thomas Cole and Jacksonian America: *The Course of Empire* as Political Allegory," *Prospects* 13 (1989), pp. 65–92.

13. R. W. Emerson, "Nature," *Emerson on Transcendentalism,* ed. E. L. Ericson (New York: Ungar, 1986), p. 5.

14. Ibid., p. 46.

15. Ibid., pp. 16–17.

16. Charles H. Brown, *William Cullen Bryant* (New York: Scribner, 1971), pp. 262–63.

17. James T. Callow, *Kindred Spirits* (Chapel Hill: University of North Carolina Press, 1967), p. 147.

18. William C. Bryant, *Poetical Works* (New York: D. Appleton and Co., 1897), pp. 63–66.

19. Ibid., pp. 37–38. Bryant's reference to the plough striking the "bare bone" may have inspired Catlin's bitter denunciation of the empire builders living in luxury "over the bones" of the slaughtered Native Americans. See George Catlin, *Letters and Notes on the Manners, Customs, and Conditions of the North American Indians*, Vol. II (Minneapolis: University of Minnesota Press, 1965), p. 256.

20. Brown, *William Cullen Bryant*, p. 283.

21. Ibid., p. 289.

22. Walt Whitman, "Our Territory on the Pacific" (July 7, 1846), *The Gathering of the Forces*, Vol. I, eds. Cleveland Rodgers and John Black (New York: G. P. Putnam's Sons, 1920), pp. 246–47.

23. Whitman, "More Stars for the Spangled Banner" (June 29, 1846), ibid., pp. 244–46.

24. Whitman, "American Futurity" (November 24, 1846), ibid., pp. 27–28.

25. Whitman, "The New World and the Old" (June 26, 1846), ibid., pp. xlii-xliii.

26. Fitz-Greene Halleck, *The Poetical Writings* (New York: Greenwood Press, 1969), p. 130. See also Nelson F. Adkins, *Fitz-Greene Halleck, An Early Knickerbocker Wit and Poet* (New Haven: Yale University Press, 1930), p. 99; James G. Wilson, *The Life and Letters of Fitz-Greene Halleck* (New York; D. Appleton and Co., 1869), p. 231.

27. Henry Thoreau, *Selected Journals*, ed. C. Bode (New York: Penguin Books, 1967), p. 171.

28. *Thoreau in the Mountains*, ed. William L. Howarth (New York: Farrar, Straus, Giroux, 1982), pp. 11–12.

29. Ibid., p. 144.

30. Ibid., p. 150.

31. Ibid., p. 40.

32. Ibid., p. 145.

33. I discuss this at length in *Art in an Age of Bonapartism* (Chicago: University of Chicago Press, 1990), Chapter 9.

34. Seth Eastman, *Treatise on Topographical Drawing* (New York: Wiley and Putnam, 1837).

35. Ibid., pp. 48–50, Plate 6, figures 1–2.

36. For an account of some of these experiences and the literature inspired by them see Marjorie H. Nicolson, *Mountain Gloom and Mountain Glory: The Development of the Aesthetics of the Infinite* (New York: Cornell University Press, 1959).

37. Thomas Hart Benton, the great-grandnephew of the Missouri expansionist, could write close to our own time, "There is a high rugged bluff above the Missouri River a few miles from Kansas City. I drive out when I get bored and sit

on that bluff. The river makes a great curve in the valley below and you can see for miles up and down the morning yel-
low water. . . . I feel very much at home looking down upon
it. Either I am just a slobbery sentimentalist or there is something to this stuff about your native land, for when I sit above
the waters of the Missouri, I feel they belong to me, and I to
them." Thomas Hart Benton, *An Artist in America* (Columbia: University of Missouri Press, 1987), p. 275.

38. Nathaniel Hawthorne, *The Marble Faun* (Boston: Tick-
nor and Fields, 1860), pp. 208–209.

39. Daryl Jones, *The Dime Novel Western* (Bowling Green,
Ohio: Popular Press, Bowling Green State University, 1978),
pp. 18–21.

40. E. S. Ellis, "Seth Jones" in *Dime Novels*, ed. E. L.
Wheeler (New York: Odyssey Press, 1966), p. 3.

41. Jones, *Dime Novel Western*, p. 19.

42. Ibid., pp. 50–51. By 1873 the heroic stage of Manifest Destiny had ended, and postbellum disillusionment had
replaced antebellum optimism. Here it may be instructive,
however, to recall that the founding father of the Daniel
Boone myth, John Filson, embedded his narrative in "an
elaborate real-estate promotion brochure" aimed at selling the
thousands of acres he secured in Kentucky country to eastern
dudes and European speculators. The Boone who led his family and others through the Cumberland Gap into the Kentucky wilderness is also Frederick Jackson Turner's archetypal
frontier hero who stands "at Cumberland Gap" and watches
"the procession of civilization." Filson prefaces his legendary
The Discovery, Settlement and Present State of Kentucke (1784)
with Boone's first sight of the fertile lands during his exploration and survey of 1769: "After a long fatiguing march, over
a mountainous wilderness, in a westward direction, they at
length arrived upon its borders; and from the top of an eminence, with joy and wonder, descried the beautiful landscape
of Kentucke." Later, in the famous appendix "The Adventures of Col. Daniel Boon," the hero recounts the primal instance of the magisterial gaze and its realization in fact:

Thus we behold Kentucke, lately an howling wilderness,
the habitation of savages and wild beasts, become a fruit-
ful field; this region, so favourably distinguished by nature, now become the habitation of civilization. . . .
Here, where the hand of violence shed the blood of the
innocent; where the horrid yells of savages, and the
groans of the distressed, sounded in our ears, we now
hear the praises and adorations of the Creator; where
wretched wigwams stood, the miserable abodes of savages, we behold the foundations of cities laid, that, in
all probability, will rival the glory of the greatest on
earth. And we view Kentucke situated on the fertile
banks of the Great Ohio, rising from obscurity to shine
with splendor, equal to any other of the stars of the
American hemisphere.

And immediately after, Boone-Filson reiterates the moment of the initial discovery when he viewed "from the top of an eminence . . . the beautiful level of Kentucke." See J. Filson, *The Discovery, Settlement and Present State of Kentucke* (New York: Corinth Books, 1962), pp. 8, 49–51; and R. Slotkin, *Regeneration Through Violence: The Mythology of the American Frontier, 1600–1860* (Middletown, Conn.: Wesleyan University Press, 1973), pp. 268–354.

43. W. G. Wall, *The Hudson River Port Folio* (New York: Henry I. Megarey, 1828), unpaginated. John Sears dates the beginnings of tourism in the United States—when there existed a wealthy strata able to travel and a body of images and descriptions to excite the imagination—from the 1820s, a date that coincides with the beginnings of the formulation of magisterial aesthetics. See John F. Sears, *Sacred Places: American Tourist Attractions in the Nineteenth Century* (New York: Oxford University Press, 1989), p. 3.

44. The most thorough exposition of the luminist school and its defenders is in *American Light: The Luminist Movement 1850–75*, ed. J. Wilmerding (Washington, D.C.: National Gallery of Art, 1980). See also G. L. Smith, "Emerson and the Luminist Painters: A Study of Their Styles," *American Quarterly* 37 (Summer 1985), pp. 193–215.

45. For Gifford we now have Ila Weiss, *Poetic Landscape: The Art and Experience of Sanford R. Gifford* (Newark: University of Delaware Press, 1987). In this respect Gifford is the most consistent of all those defined as luminists, framing vast aerial spaces in his views of the Catskills from South Mountain.

46. The diminishing, but not the elimination, of the focused gaze in Kensett, Heade, and Fitz Hugh Lane and the undeclinated view of the panorama are inseparable from the diminishing of the energy of the drive for Manifest Destiny in the wake of the Civil War and the onset of a nostalgic point of view. This younger generation has come to take Manifest Destiny for granted, as an objective part of their existence, no longer a hoped-for ideal. They buy and sell real estate, own railroad shares, and paint the land they own or the views surrounding it. Already the government is setting aside wilderness sites for conservation like large-scale Central Parks, beginning the process of looking at nature as if it were a diorama. Once Manifest Destiny has been achieved it is possible to think of preserving pockets of wilderness for the delectation of the public. Hence the change in the perspective of this generation. The scenery is now a fait accompli, objective, fixed part of the horizon, subsumed to their actual control and sense of control. The sense of flattening out actually gives me a greater sense of a stage set than the stagier works of Cole and Durand. Futurity has in fact arrived and can now be suppressed. The woods have been cleared along with the wilderness foreground, and therefore the unencumbered view and absent brushwork signify a more finished state of the landscape. No imaginary pathways through the

wilderness make sense now, because they are already a marked part of the landscape. In short, the so-called luminists pave the way for a more cosmopolitan approach, one no longer homebound, because the nation is secure in its geographical and political boundaries. Now painters can turn once again to Europe for inspiration, and the patrons can turn their backs on the likes of Bierstadt and Church. Only a Thomas Moran can survive this evolution in taste because his immense views of inaccessible places are geared to the sense of preserved sites and railroad tourism. The image of the West continues, but in its nostalgic expression as an ideal of Anglo-Saxon militance in the face of East European immigration and the growth of an organized labor force.

47. The book was a favorite of William Cullen Bryant's: see J. F. Cooper, *The Pioneers* (London: Dent, 1929), p. vii.

48. Ibid., pp. 170–200.

49. Ibid., pp. 268–69.

50. Ibid., pp. 1–2.

51. Ibid., p. 30.

52. Ibid., p. 223.

53. For the background to this work see R. H. Stehle, "Westward Ho! The History of Leutze's Fresco in the Capitol," *Records of the Columbia Historical Society,* Washington, D.C., 1970–1972, pp. 306–22; Barbara S. Groseclose, *Emanuel Leutze, 1816–1868: Freedom Is the Only King* (Washington, D.C.: Smithsonian Institution Press, 1975), pp. 60–62.

54. E. Lies, "Westward, Ho!" *The United States Magazine and Democratic Review,* new series, Vol. 24 (January 1849), p. 43.

55. J. Gray Sweeney, *The Artist-Explorers of the American West 1860–1880* (Ph.D. dissertation, Indiana University, 1975), p. 58.

56. Patricia A. Anderson, *The Course of Empire: The Erie Canal and the New York Landscape, 1825–1875* (Rochester, N.Y.: Memorial Art Gallery of the University of Rochester, 1984), p. 13.

57. Quoted in John K. Howat, *The Hudson River and Its Painters* (New York: Viking Press, 1972) pp. 34–35.

58. Huth, *Nature and the American*, p. 77. See also Alan Wallach's "Making a Picture of the View from Mount Holyoke," which I have seen only in manuscript. Wallach studies the work in the context of the panorama and sees the spatial location as a metaphor analogous to the Foucauldian notion of the panopticon—but now the viewer assumes the position of the supreme authority.

59. Nathaniel Parker Willis, *American Scenery* (Barre, Mass.: Imprint Society, 1971, originally published 1840), pp. 14–16.

60. Ibid., p. 16.

61. See G. H. Williams, *Wilderness and Paradise in Christian Thought* (New York: Harper, 1962).

62. Wadsworth began systematically acquiring tracts of land on top of Talcott Mountain in Avon (then part of Farmington) around 1805, and by 1848 the estate comprised

250 acres on a peak affording panoramic views in all directions. See R. Saunders, *Daniel Wadsworth, Patron of the Arts* (Hartford, Conn.: Wadsworth Atheneum, 1981), pp. 17–29.

63. Noble, *Life and Works of Thomas Cole*, pp. 66–67.

64. Ibid., pp. 372–73.

65. Ibid., p. 241.

66. Willis, *American Scenery*, p. 3.

67. Ibid., p. 83.

68. Ibid., pp. 101–104.

69. Ibid., pp. 152–54.

70. Ibid., pp. 157–58.

71. See the discussion in Franklin Kelly, *Frederic Edwin Church and the National Landscape* (Washington, D.C.: Smithsonian Institution Press, 1988), pp. 68–72.

72. Kelly sees this as Church's nostalgic concern for the wilderness, while I see it as consistent with the main body of his work and the taste of his patrons; ibid., pp. 115–16.

73. See David C. Huntington, *The Landscapes of Frederic Edwin Church: Vision of an American Era* (New York: G. Braziller, 1966), pp. 67–68; essays by Jeremy E. Adamson and E. McKinsey, in *Niagara: Two Centuries of Changing Attitudes, 1697–1901*, ed. Adamson (Washington, D.C.: Corcoran Gallery of Art, 1985), pp. 11–101.

74. Adam Badeau, *The Vagabond* (New York: Rudd and Carleton, 1859), p. 123.

75. Quoted in Adamson, *Niagara*, p. 67.

76. W. D. Hoyt, "Documents. Journey to Niagara, 1815," *New York History* 32 (1942), pp. 331, 334. Typically, Willis recommends for "the seasoned traveller" the view from the terraces of the exclusive Niagara hotel known as the Clifton House, where one could endlessly calculate "the force, speed, and change of the tremendous waters" and provide oneself with "amusement and occupation enough to draw the mind from anything,—to cure madness or create it." *American Scenery*, pp. 66–68.

77. Huntington, *Landscapes of Frederic Edwin Church*, p. 5; Kelly, *Frederic Edwin Church*, p. 99.

78. See Manthorne, *Creation and Renewal*, p. 7, on Cotopaxi (1862).

79. Whitman exulted in an editorial for the Brooklyn *Daily Times* that the laying of the cable represented "the union of the great Anglo-Saxon race, henceforth forever to be a unit," and wrote that this event "thrills every breast with admiration and triumph." Whitman, "The Moral Effect of the Cable" (August 16, 1858), *I Sit and Look Out*, p. 159.

80. Manthorne, *Creation and Renewal*, pp. 52–56; J. P. Harrison, "Science and Politics: Origins and Objectives of Mid-Nineteenth Century Government Expeditions to Latin America," *Hispanic American Historical Review* 35 (1955), pp. 175–202.

81. Huntington, *Landscapes of Frederic Edwin Church*, p. 42.

82. S. Carter III, *Cyrus Field: Man of Two Worlds* (New York: Putnam, 1968), pp. 65–66.

83. Ibid., pp. 49–50; Kelly, *Frederic Edwin Church*, p. 16.

84. Carter, *Cyrus Field*, p. 50.

85. Isabella F. Judson, *Cyrus W. Field: His Life and Work (1819–1892)* (New York: Harper and Brothers, 1896), p. 40.

86. Carter, *Cyrus Field*, pp. 79–80. See the *Daily National Intelligencer* November 17, 19, 27 (includes letters III and IV), 29, December 1, and 3, 1852.

87. Jaquelin A. Caskie, *Life and Letters of Matthew Fontaine Maury* (Richmond, Va.: Richmond Press, 1928), pp. 52–79.

88. Maury, "Southern and Western Commerce," *Daily National Intelligencer* February 4, 1852.

89. Maury ("Inca"), "The Amazon and the Atlantic Slopes of South America," *Daily National Intelligencer* November 17, 1852.

90. Caskie, *Life and Letters*, p. 122; Maury, "The Amazon and the Atlantic Slopes," December 3, 1852. See also Katherine E. Manthorne, *Tropical Renaissance: North American Artists Exploring Latin America, 1839–1879* (Washington, D.C.: Smithsonian Institution Press, 1989), pp. 52–53.

91. Maury, "The Amazon and the Atlantic Slopes," December 3, 1852.

92. Judson, *Cyrus W. Field*, pp. 52–53; Manthorne, *Tropical Renaissance*, p. 75; *American Paradise: The World of the Hudson River School* (New York: Metropolitan Museum of Art, 1987), p. 248.

93. Judson, *Cyrus W. Field*, pp. 54–55.

94. Maury, "The Amazon and the Atlantic Slopes," November 17, 1852.

95. Judson, *Cyrus W. Field*, p. 56.

96. Carter, *Cyrus Field*, p. 87.

97. Ibid., pp. 257–63; Judson, *Cyrus W. Field*, pp. 211–31; Henry Martin Field, *The Story of the Atlantic Telegraph* (New York: Scribner's Sons, 1893), pp. iii–v.

98. Judson, *Cyrus W. Field*, pp. 61–62.

99. Ibid., pp. 74–75; J. Mullaly, *The Laying of the Cable, or The Ocean Telegraph* (New York: D. Appleton and Co., 1858), pp. 18–21; Field, *Story of the Atlantic Telegraph*, pp. 18–21, 66–72; Carter, *Cyrus Field*, pp. 97–120.

100. Walt Whitman, "The Moral Effect of the Cable," *I Sit and Look Out: Editorials from the Brooklyn Daily Times*, eds. E. Holloway and V. Schwarz (New York: Columbia University Press, 1932), pp. 159–161.

101. Carter, *Cyrus Field*, pp. 267–94, 327.

102. Ibid., p. 328.

103. Huntington, *Landscapes of Frederic Edwin Church*, pp. 114ff.; P. L. Goss, *An Investigation of Olana, the Home of Frederic Edwin Church, Painter* (Ph.D. dissertation, Ohio State University, 1973); Franklin Kelly and G. L. Carr, *The Early Landscapes of Frederic Edwin Church, 1845–1854* (Fort Worth: Amon Carter Museum, 1987).

104. Huntington, *Landscapes of Frederic Edwin Church*, pp. 114–16.

105. See the discussion of K. W. Maddox, "Asher B. Durand's *Progress:* The Advance of Civilization and the Vanishing American," in *The Railroad in American Art: Representations of Technological Change,* eds. Susan Danly and Leo Marx (Cambridge, Mass.: MIT Press, 1988), pp. 51–69.

106. "Exhibition of the National Academy of Design," *The Knickerbocker* 42 (July 1853), p. 95.

107. Patricia Trenton and Peter H. Hassrick, *The Rocky Mountains: A Vision for Artists in the Nineteenth Century* (Norman: University of Oklahoma Press, 1983), pp. 73–74.

108. Quoted in Robert L. Gale, *Thomas Crawford, American Sculptor* (Pittsburgh: University of Pittsburgh Press, 1964), p. 109.

109. Ibid., pp. 111–12.

110. Anderson, *Course of Empire,* pp. 46–47.

111. Quoted in Novak, *Nature and Culture,* p. 5.

112. A. B. Durand, "Letters on Landscape Painting," *Crayon* 1 (1854–55), letter IV, pp. 97–98.

113. Ibid., letter II, pp. 34–35.

114. For discussions of the work see Callow, *Kindred Spirits,* pp. 67–68; David B. Lawall, *Asher Brown Durand: His Art and Art Theory in Relation to His Times* (New York: Garland, 1977), pp. 516ff.

115. *The Home Book of the Picturesque* (New York: George P. Putnam, 1852). For background on this publication, see Callow, *Kindred Spirits,* pp. 169–70.

116. *Home Book,* p. vii.

117. See the chauvinistic claptrap of G. M. Bethune, "Art in the United States," ibid., pp. 167–88.

118. Stehle, "Westward Ho!" pp. 311–12.

119. E. L. Magoon, "Scenery and Mind," *Home Book,* pp. 1–48.

120. Ibid., p. 5.

121. Ibid., p. 6.

122. Ibid., pp. 9–10.

123. Ibid., pp. 26–27.

124. Ibid., p. 27.

125. Ibid., p. 34.

126. Ibid., p. 36.

127. Ibid., pp. 38–47.

128. J. F. Cooper, "American and European Scenery Compared," *Home Book,* pp. 51–69.

29. Ibid., p. 56.

130. Ibid., pp. 53–54.

131. Ibid., p. 61.

132. Miss Cooper (sic), "A Dissolving Mist," *Home Book,* pp. 79–94.

133. Ibid., pp. 81–83.

134. H. T. Tuckerman, "Over the Mountains, or the Western Pioneer," *Home Book,* pp. 115–35.

135. Ibid., p. 117. For discussions and a reproduction of the work, see D. Glanz, *The Iconography of Westward Expansion*

in American Art, 1820–70: Selected Topics (Ph.D. dissertation, University of North Carolina at Chapel Hill, 1978), pp. 30–32; W. H. Truettner, "The Art of History: American Exploration and Discovery Scenes, 1840–60," *American Art Journal* 14 (Winter 1982), pp. 25–26.

136. Bayard Taylor, "The Scenery of Pennsylvania," *Home Book,* pp. 95–103; "The Erie Railroad," *Home Book,* pp. 143–54. Most recently, Taylor's relationship to the landscapists has been discussed in Weiss, *Poetic Landscape,* pp. 21–45.

137. Bayard Taylor, *Life and Letters* Vol. I, eds. M. Hansen-Taylor and H. E. Scudder (Boston: Houghton, Mifflin, 1895), pp. 169, 201.

138. Taylor had been one of the select group of writers and artists to make the highly publicized excursion over the Erie Railroad in 1849. Ibid., p. 141. There would be many more to follow in the coming years as the railroads lured the intellectuals into promoting the scenery along their routes to encourage tourism.

139. Taylor, "The Erie Railroad," *Home Book,* p. 144.

140. Ibid., p. 145.

141. See John Tomsich, *A Genteel Endeavor: American Culture and Politics in the Gilded Age* (Stanford: Stanford University Press, 1971), pp. 27–50.

142. Bayard Taylor, *A Journey to Central Africa* (New York: G. P. Putnam's Sons, 1879), p. 327.

143. J. R. Schultz, *The Unpublished Letters of Bayard Taylor in the Huntington Library* (San Marino, Calif.: Huntington Library Publications, 1937), p. 31.

144. *American Paradise,* pp. 185, 250.

145. Carter, *Cyrus Field,* pp. 113–14, 302; Manthorne, *Tropical Renaissance,* p. 120.

146. Bayard Taylor, *At Home and Abroad: A Sketch-Book of Life, Scenery and Men* (New York: G. P. Putnam, 1862), pp. 344–45.

147. Ibid., pp. 360–61.

148. Tomsich, *A Genteel Endeavor,* pp. 45–46.

149. Taylor, *At Home and Abroad,* pp. 3–19.

150. Albert H. Smyth, *Bayard Taylor* (Detroit: Gale Research Co., 1970, facsimile of 1896 edition), pp. 105, 141.

151. Taylor, *At Home and Abroad,* p. 7.

152. Ibid., p. 8.

153. Ibid., p. 9.

154. Ibid., pp. 12–13.

155. Ibid., pp. 13–14.

156. Ibid., pp. 15–16. Taylor also grouped among those excluded "those who worship the golden calf," a curious assertion from one whose whole life had been guided by the same veneration. He kept accepting Putnam's offers to edit works just for the money and lectured extensively despite the toll on his time and health because "he knew well that in no

other way could he so quickly reach the independence of fortune which was his goal." See Taylor, *Life and Letters* Vol. I, pp. 201, 291, 344.

157. Taylor, *At Home and Abroad*, p. 17.

158. Bayard Taylor, *Views Afoot, or Europe Seen with a Knapsack and Staff* (New York: G. P. Putnam, 1902), pp. 99–100.

159. Taylor, *At Home and Abroad*, p. 118.

160. Ibid., p. 171.

161. Ibid., p. 41.

162. Ibid., pp. 59–60.

163. *American Paradise*, pp. 206–207.

164. Ibid., p. 206.

165. Ibid., pp. 208–210.

166. *Saturday Evening Post*, March 6, 1926, p. 97.

167. Donald H. Cresswell, *The American Revolution in Drawings and Prints* (Washington, D.C.: Library of Congress, 1975), Nos. 494, 500, 525–26, 546–47, 551–52, 557.

168. L. Parry, "Landscape Theater in America," *Art in America* 59 (November-December 1971), pp. 57–58. The major work on the history of the panorama is S. Oettermann, *Das Panorama, Die Geschichte eines Massenmediums* (Frankfurt am Main: Syndikat Autoren und Verlagsgesellschaft, 1980), pp. 9–40. Oettermann notes that the panorama was a surrogate for mountain peak experience.

169. See Novak, *Nature and Culture*, pp. 175–76; Taft, *Artists and Illustrators*, pp. 149–50; Trenton and Hassrick, *Rocky Mountains*, p. 78; Danly and Marx, *Railroad in American Art*, pp. 5–30.

170. Leo Marx, "The Railroad-in-the-Landscape: An Iconological Reading of a Theme in American Art," Danly and Marx, *Railroad in American Art*, pp. 198–99. For the fuller exposition of his theory of the middle landscape, see Marx's *The Machine in the Garden* (New York: Oxford University Press, 1964), pp. 139ff. See the excellent review of this railroad literature in D. Lubin, "A Backward Look at Forward Motion," *American Quarterly* 41 (September 1989), pp. 549–57. See also A. F. Hyde, *An American Vision: Far Western Landscape and National Culture, 1820–1920* (New York: New York University Press, 1990), Chapter 2.

171. Marx, *Machine in the Garden*, p. 220; N. Cikovsky, Jr., "George Inness and the Hudson River School: The Lackawanna Valley," *American Art Journal* 2 (Fall 1970), pp. 36–57; N. Cikovsky, Jr., "George Inness's *The Lackawanna Valley*: 'Type of the Modern'," Danly and Marx, *Railroad in American Art*, pp. 71–91.

172. *Acts of the Legislatures of the States of Pennsylvania and New York Relating to the Delaware, Lackawanna, and Western Railroad Company* (New York: John F. Trow, 1856), pp. 58, 84–85.

173. Ibid., p. 84.

174. Trenton and Hassrick, *Rocky Mountains*, p. 67.

175. Donald Jackson and M. L. Spence, eds., *The Expeditions of John Charles Frémont*, Vol. I (Urbana: University of Illinois Press, 1970–1984), pp. xvii-xviii; Smith, *Virgin Land*, pp. 23–25; Herman J. Viola, *Exploring the West* (Washington, D.C.: Smithsonian Books, 1987), pp. 65, 107.

176. Jackson and Spence, *Expeditions of John Charles Frémont*, p. 270.

177. Ibid., Vol. III, pp. xxi-xxii.

178. Ibid., Vol. I, pp. xxvi, xxix; Viola, *Exploring the West*, p. 107.

179. Viola, *Exploring the West*, p. 109.

180. Taft, *Artists and Illustrators*, p. 5; Trenton and Hassrick, *Rocky Mountains*, p. 74. The most important work on the links between the expeditions and their impact on American culture generally is W. H. Goetzmann, *Exploration and Empire* (New York: Norton, 1966).

181. A contemporary description of the work is found in George A. Crofutt, *Crofutt's New Overland Tourist and Pacific Coast Guide* (Chicago: Overland Publishing Co., 1878–1879), p. 300.

182. R. S. Trump, *Life and Works of Albert Bierstadt* (Ph.D. dissertation, Ohio State University, 1963), p. 130.

183. Ibid., p. 78; Gordon Hendricks, *Albert Bierstadt, Painter of the American West* (New York: H. N. Abrams, 1988), pp. 116–36.

184. F. H. Ludlow, *The Heart of the Continent: A Record of Travel Across the Plains and in Oregon with an Examination of the Mormon Principle* (New York: Hurd and Houghton, 1870), pp. 426–33.

185. Hendricks, *Albert Bierstadt*, p. 58. Not surprisingly, Taylor, N. P. Willis, and John C. Frémont became important fans and patrons of the painter. Ibid., pp. 100, 113, 158.

186. Ibid., p. 233.

187. Ibid., pp. 167–72.

188. Sweeney, *Artist-Explorers of the American West*, pp. 275–77.

189. J. R. Stilgoe, *Common Landscape of America, 1580–1845* (New Haven: Yale University Press, 1982), pp. 98–105.

190. Jackson and Spence, *Expeditions of John Charles Frémont*, Vol. I, p. xxi.

191. Ibid., p. xxx.

192. G. M. Wheeler, *Report upon the United States Geographical Surveys West of the One-Hundredth Meridian* (Washington, D.C.: Government Printing Office, 1889) p. 35.

193. Ibid., p. 214.

194. Ibid., p. 219.

195. Clarence King, *Mountaineering in the Sierra Nevada*

(Lincoln: University of Nebraska Press, 1970), p. 40.

196. Ibid., p. 274.

197. Viola, *Exploring the West*, pp. 136–70.

198. F. V. Hayden, *Geological Report of the Exploration of the Yellowstone and Missouri Rivers* (Washington, D.C.: Government Printing Office, 1869), p. viii.

199. F. V. Hayden, *The Great West: Its Attractions and Resources* (Bloomington, Ill.: C. R. Brodix, 1880).

200. T. L. Karnes, *William Gilpin, Western Nationalist* (Austin: University of Texas Press, 1970), p. 305. See also Hyde, *An American Vision*, pp. 31–33.

201. Ibid., pp. 306–12.

202. Quoted in Viola, *Exploring the West*, p. 156.

203. Karnes, *William Gilpin*, pp. 51–92.

204. Jackson and Spence, *Expeditions of John Charles Frémont*, Vol. I, p. 430. Frémont described him as a "useful and agreeable addition to the party."

205. Karnes, *William Gilpin*, p. 239.

206. Ibid.

207. William Gilpin, *Notes on Colorado* (London: British Association of Science, 1870), p. 6.

208. William Gilpin, *Mission of the North American People* (New York: Da Capo Press, 1974, reprint of 1860 edition), p. 8.

209. Ibid., pp. ix-x, 15–22, 42. The Isothermal Zodiac is Gilpin's belt, thirty degrees in average width across the Northern Hemisphere, that passes through the oceans at their narrowest and the continents at their widest points. In this zone lives 95 percent of the white race, and within it the most advanced cultures have sprung up. See also Smith, *Virgin Land*, pp. 42–44.

210. Gilpin, *Mission of the North American People*, p. 121.

211. Ibid., pp. 61–62.

212. Gilpin, *Notes on Colorado*, p. 5.

213. T. Poesche and C. Goepp, *The New Rome; or, The United States of the World* (New York: G. P. Putnam and Co., 1853), p. 11.

214. C. W. Wendte, *Thomas Starr King, Patriot and Preacher* (Boston: Beacon Press, 1921), pp. 172–73.

215. T. Starr King, *The White Hills: Their Legends, Landscape and Poetry* (Boston: Crosby, Nichols, and Co., 1860), pp. 34, 169, 176, 270, 342.

216. Gilpin, *Mission of the North American People*, p. 70.

217. Gilpin, *Notes on Colorado*, pp. 45–46.

218. Jackson and Spence, *Expeditions of John Charles Frémont*, p. 5.

219. King, *Mountaineering in the Sierra Nevada*, p. 276.

220. Ibid., p. 238.

221. Ibid., pp. 238–39.

222. Jackson and Spence, *Expeditions of John Charles Frémont*, Vol. I, p. 270.

223. N. P. Langford, *Diary of the Washburn Expedition to the Yellowstone and Firehole Rivers in the Year 1870* (St. Paul, Minn., 1905), pp. 96–97.

224. J. M. Sganzin, *An Elementary Course of Civil Engineering* (Boston: Hilliard, Gray, and Co., 1837), pp. 104–105.

225. I have found useful C. Singer and E. J. Holmyard, et al., eds., *A History of Technology* IV: The Industrial Revolution c. 1750 to c. 1850 (Oxford: Clarendon Press, 1958), pp. 605–608; F. H. Moffitt and H. Bouchard, *Surveying* (New York: Harper and Row, 1987), pp. 369–85.

226. H. Gannett, *The Aims and Methods of Cartography* (Baltimore: Johns Hopkins Press, 1898), p. 251.

227. I studied the triangulation records of the geological survey of the 1880s, and almost invariably the surveyor chose the "highest summit" in the area for a station. National Archives and Records Administration (NARA), Topographic Division, RG 57, Records of the Geological Survey, Triangulation Record Books, seventeen volumes, 1882–1906. I was especially interested in the volume entitled "Triangulation, Indian Territory."

228. Trenton and Hassrick, *Rocky Mountains*, pp. 44–45.

229. Ibid., p. 78.

230. For example, in the triangulation records of the geological survey it is often noted that the stations are cleared "and one tree left for a signal," or in one case a signal was "made from three large fir trees, over big rock on summit." NARA, vol. 1, pp. 38, 41.

231. John Durand, *The Life and Times of A. B. Durand* (New York: C. Scribner's Sons, 1894), pp. 30ff.

232. R. A. Smith, *The Carving of Mount Rushmore* (New York: Abbeville Press, 1985), p. 96.

233. L. Borglum, *Mount Rushmore: The Story Behind the Scenery* (Las Vegas: KC Publications, 1977), p. 13.

234. Letter from Borglum to Battle, September 27, 1932, Gutzon Borglum Papers, Library of Congress, Manuscript Division, Washington, D.C.

235. Borglum, *Mount Rushmore*, p. 48.

236. Letter from Mary Borglum to "The Answer Man," July 25, 1949, Gutzon Borglum Papers.

237. G. C. Fite, *Mount Rushmore* (Norman: University of Oklahoma Press, 1952), pp. 34–35.

238. D. Robinson, *A History of the Dakota or Sioux Indians* (Minneapolis: Ross and Haines, 1956), pp. 408–13.

239. John Fire (Lame Deer) and R. Erdoes, *Lame Deer, Seeker of Visions* (New York: Simon and Schuster, 1972), p. 93.

Index

Fig. 17. Reproduced in *Cyrus W. Field: His Life and Work*, by Isabella F. Judson (New York: Harper, 1896), opposite p. 124.

Figs. 22 and 23. Prints and Photographs Division, Library of Congress, Washington, D.C.

Fig. 25. Reproduced in *Harper's Weekly*, 29 June 1878.

Fig. 34. Reproduced in *Graham's Magazine*, June 1848.

Fig. 45. Reproduced in *The Aims and Methods of Cartography*, by Henry Gannett (Baltimore: Johns Hopkins University Press), p. 251.